WOMEN AGAINST APARTHEID: THE FIGHT FOR FREEDOM IN SOUTH AFRICA, 1920-1975

BY: NANCY VAN VUUREN

PALO ALTO, CALIFORNIA
1979

PUBLISHED BY

R & E RESEARCH ASSOCIATES, INC.
936 INDUSTRIAL AVENUE
PALO ALTO, CALIFORNIA 94303

PUBLISHERS

ROBERT D. REED AND ADAM S. ETEROVICH

Library of Congress Card Catalog Number

78-62222

I.S.B.N.

0-88247-575-4

TABLE OF CONTENTS

PREFACE

The search for information on the role of women in the anti-apartheid movement in South Africa is especially difficult since everyone opposed to apartheid ("separate development" for people of each race) is a threat to the Government. Any action or word can be interpreted as ground for arrest, detention, even torture. I have, therefore, been careful both not to contact women who could suffer because of such an inquiry and not to include information which could be used to hurt anyone. Individual women hold a wealth of information which cannot be included, but the material which is here suggests the role of women is so vital to the anti-apartheid movement that without them the movement would have been but a shell.

This information was gathered piece by piece from a myriad of sources over a long period of time. Together the pieces form the shape of the puzzle, but much of the body yet remains to be filled in. Because the individual pieces are so tiny, I have not documented them except where they come from one source only, or are quotations. The bibliography lists all the sources which were used.

As the introductory sections on the development of South Africa and on the status of women in South Africa show, the roles of women in South Africa are similar to those of women throughout the rest of the world. The Government and the tribal leaders expected women to be subordinate to men, to have children and to be responsible for raising them, to earn less pay than men even if in the same job class, and to fill the majority of nursing, teaching, secretarial, and domestic service positions. Through these expectations men, white and black, separated women from the normal political, educational, legal, and economic structures and decision-making. Women, therefore, built their own society and their own lines of communication. These were traditionally viewed as unimportant by the men. But periodically the women would impose themselves on the male society with demands and organizational strength which the men had never suspected was there, and which the men could never themselves attain except as they held the traditional positions of power. When this occurred, the men would either tolerate the women's actions or attempt to crush them with direct force, but they never came to understand the separate society nor to respond to it.

Because the society of women concerned itself with day to day living - housing, food, education, medical care - the women might be described as experts in survival. In a social structure built on suppression of the majority of the people, including everyone who does not identify with those in power, survival skills become paramount. More than that, though, the separate communication and social system that women had developed provided the functional basis for their anti-Government, anti-apartheid actions.

The thesis is, therefore, that not only did women have a part in the anti-apartheid movement, but, without them, there would have been no mass movement. This is not to deny that men consistently filled the official leadership positions. Such was "normal" to a male-dominated society, and the Government could never have dealt with a female leadership. But the organization, the involvement of the people, the raising of basic issues, came from the unofficial and unrecognized society established and run by the women.

This generalized thesis applies to all racial groups. Because the white men controlled the "legitimate" power in the country, they felt the force of the women only when they opposed the Government and the economic power structure. Black men felt the power of the women in their ability to identify issues and problems and to take action to deal with them. Because the women had no point of access to those in power, they could not expect resolution of problems through meetings and discussions. And they knew that a level of commitment would be required which could mean destruction of what little they had managed to achieve, but for many of them there was no choice.

The functions and bonds of this women's society were probably not consciously known to the women except as they experienced a bond in their own anti-apartheid actions. These women did not have to be feminists, but they did have to rebel against their own oppression and against the controls which the male-dominated society imposed on them. And the women active in the anti-apartheid movement were aware of the strength they had together. In working and organizing for common goals they achieved a knowledge of each other and a closeness which the men never experienced. It is because of this common bond and action that I have not singled out a few individuals, but rather have tried to reveal the broad involvement of many women leaders in the opposition to apartheid.

I am not suggesting that what the men did was unimportant. And I do not deal with the men's activities or leadership roles. However, I am saying that in this particular situation effective action by men was impossible because they were already a part of one power hierarchy, that of men (i.e. some African and Colored men could vote long before any women could vote.) Race discrimination excluded black men. It also excluded black women. And sex discrimination excluded all women even from areas into which black men were allowed.

The official and the recognized leadership of the anti-apartheid movement came from men. But the unofficial leadership came from women - Afrikaner and African women trade union organizers, the African National Congress Women's League, the women leaders of the Coloured and Indian communities, the Federation of South African Women, the Black Sash, the women of the South African Institute of Race Relations, and the women of the Congress of Democrats and of the Communist Party.

VI

ACRONYMNS

AMWU	African Mine Workers' Union
ANC	African National Congress
ARM	African Resistance Movement (Seventies)
BPC	Black People's Convention
BCP	Black Community Programmes
CI	Communist International
CPSA	Communist Party of South Africa (1921-1950)
COD	Congress of Democrats
COP	Congress of the People (1955)
DRC	Dutch Reformed Church
DWEP	Domestic Workers and Employers' Project
FAK	Federasie van Afrikaanse Kultuurverenigings (Federation of Afrikaner Cultural Organizations)
FOFATUSA	Federation of Free African Trade Unions of South Africa
GDP	Gross Domestic Product
GWU	Garment Workers' Union
ICA	Industrial Conciliation Act
ICWU/ICU	Industrial and Commercial Workers Union
ILO	International Labor Organization
NCW	National Council of Women
NEUF	Non-European Unity Front (1938-)
NEUM	Non-European Unity Movement (1943-)
NTUF	Non-European Trade Union Federation
NUSAS	National Union of South African Students
PAC	Pan African Congress
SACP	South African Communist Party (1953-)
SACTU	South African Congress of Trade Unions
SACPO	South African Colored People's Organization
SAIC	South African Indian Congress
SAIRR	South African Institute of Race Relations
SALP	South African Labor Party
SASO	South African Students Organization
SATUC	South African Trade Union Congress (1926-1930)
SAT&LC	South African Trades and Labor Council (1930-1954)
SCA	Suppression of Communism Act (1950-)
SEIFSA	Steel and Engineering Industries Federation of South Africa
SPRO-CAS	Study Project On Christianity in Apartheid Society
TUCSA	Trade Union Council of South Africa (1954-)
UP	United Party
USP	United Socialist Party

GLOSSARY

APARTHEID	"separate development" for people of each race
BANNING	action taken by the Minister of Justice, under provisions of the Suppression of Communism Act as amended, to restrict an individual's movement, activities, association, and publication
BLACK	not white, including Africans, Indians, other Asians, and Coloreds; came into use in the late sixties
COLOR BAR	used to describe the reservation of certain job classes for persons of a particular race
EXIT PERMIT	document allowing a person to leave South Africa legally
HOMELAND	area of land set aside for persons of a particular ancestry (tribe)
INFLUX	movement of blacks into urban areas or areas in which whites predominate
KWASHIORKOR	disease caused by malnutrition
PASS	documents required to be kept on one's person at all times when outside one's home; define a person's legal and racial status; required only of blacks
RAND	currency, approximately equivalent to U.S. $1.40
RESERVE	cf homeland
REFERENCE BOOK	replaced the myriad of documents known as the pass, combining them into one book
MULTI-RACIAL OR MIXED	including persons of different races
CONGRESS MOVEMENT OR ALLIANCE	coordinated activities of the ANC, SAIC, SACPO, COD, SACTU, and the Federation of South African Women
BANTU EDUCATION (NATIONAL CHRISTIAN EDUCATION)	Afrikaner Nationalist controlled education having the philosophy of white supremacy and emphasizing Afrikaner culture
LISTED	i.e. as a Communist under the Suppression of Communism Act
BORDER INDUSTRY	factory located in a white area near an African Reserve, away from the urban areas, which employs Africans living in that Reserve

CHAPTER 1

I. INTRODUCTION

Most people think of South Africa as some strange nation in
which the white minority rigidly controls the black majority, an
anachronism out of colonial times. This image is not totally
incorrect, but what it lacks is the reality of day to day life
for the 21,000,000 people who are South Africans. Besides being
African, Colored, Asian, and white (English and Afrikaner)[+],
these people are male and female. And much as racial segregation
and oppression have been publicized, little attention has been
paid to the women of South Africa.

Thousands of women have been activists in the efforts to
obtain equality and justice for every South African. To understand the role that women played, however, it is necessary to
first review briefly the history of South Africa prior to 1920
and the overall status of women.

[+]The racial categories used throughout will be the same
as those used by the South African Government, in order
of status, lowest to highest:
> African, Native - a person whose origins were in an
African tribe
> Colored - mixed African and white, including many
descendants or the first Dutch settlers
> Asian - mainly Indians, "imported" originally to
work in the sugar cane fields in Natal
> Non-European, non-white, black - all of the above
> White - mainly of Afrikaner (Dutch/Boer) or English
descent, meeting certain qualifications in color of skin,
facial features, hair texture
> European - white
All of the above labels will be capitalized except black
and white, both of which are generally accepted as not
being proper nouns. The other labels either have a
narrow definition in South African usage or refer to the
name of a continent, and so are capitalized.

Though for decades South African historians and Government
apologists declared that African tribes and Dutch merchants
arrived in the geographical area known as South Africa at about
the same time, recent archeological evidence and historical
research suggest the African tribes arrived long before the "white
man." When the Dutch sailors arrived in 1652 - all men -, they
established the Cape Colony as a trading post and stopping place
for merchant ships. The sailors took local girls/women as mis-
tresses and wives, shortly creating the "Cape Colored" population.
Local men and women, mainly Hottentots, performed labor for the
new settlers, and gradually became dependent on them for income

1

and goods. As the colony grew, more and more Africans from surrounding areas were drawn into service. At the same time the
white settlers began to reach out and claim more and more land and
to import slaves.

The British first tried to annex the Cape in 1781 and their
first occupation took place from 1795-1803. A process similar to
that followed in the settling of the American West ensued. But
while the white American tried to remove or exterminate the Indian,
the white South African used the African as servant and cheap
labor. The frontier battles for land, the tribal wars, the trading
of liquor and firearms, the escape from government, the attitude
of white superiority, were all much the same. Following several
wars Holland ceded the Cape to Britain (1814) and in 1820, 5,000
British settlers arrived. In 1834 the British Parliament officially abolished slavery. And by 1843 the new Republic of Natal
had also become a British colony.

The Afrikaner Great Trek which began from the Cape in 1836
was the Afrikaners' effort to be free of English rule and domination, and became the focal point of Afrikaner Nationalism. Through
the Trek and the many battles with African tribes the Afrikaners
"settled," laid claim to, what later became the Transvaal and the
Orange Free State, the "Boer Republics." In 1844 the majority of
Afrikaners/Boers in Natal left for the new Boer Republics.

With the discovery of diamonds on the Rand in the Transvaal
in 1867, change was forced upon the rural Afrikaners. The British
wanted to gain control of the diamond fields, and officially
annexed them in 1870. Fortune hunters flocked to the Rand. Then
in 1877 Britain claimed the Transvaal as British territory. Urban
areas began to develop, and the rural frontier society of the
Afrikaner was disrupted. Then in 1886 the Witwatersrand (in the
Transvaal) gold fields were opened.

The whites, English and Afrikaner, thus simply declared entire
regions to belong to them. If anyone opposed them, they became
subject to white law or white arms. Such arrogance was not peculiar
to whites in South Africa, but typical of 19th century colonialism.

With settlement, industrialization, and urbanization came the
traditional English/Dutch need for some form of administrative,
legislative, and judicial controls. Every community has to establish and enforce rules, but the 1880s brought a number of crises
in South Africa which forced the formation of complex governmental
structures. In this process emerged the widespread intent to make
all non-whites less than full citizens. The Cape at that time did
allow the franchise to certain Coloreds and Africans (male, with
specific income and education levels) and did uphold in theory
"equality of every person before the law." But in all four republics (Natal, Cape, Transvaal, and Orange Free State) laws were
passed to limit the citizenship of non-whites. No woman, of any
race, had the right to vote or to hold public office.

Given the small number of whites as compared to non-whites,
it is somewhat surprising that the whites would allow themselves
the luxury of the battle for power known as the Boer War, 1899-1902.
(Again note the parallel to colonial wars in America.) The
Afrikaners/Voortrekkers wanted independence from Great Britain,

and Great Britain was at the height of her colonial power, eager to claim all of South Africa and all the mineral wealth. At the end of the Boer War, under the Treaty of Vereeniging of 1902, both Afrikaner Republics (Transvaal and Orange Free State) became British colonies.

The wounds experienced by the Afrikaners in the Boer War have never healed. Just as the Afrikaners treated Africans as non-citizens, so did the English-speaking treat the Afrikaners. The formation of the Union of South Africa in 1910, the result of conciliation efforts by the English, with Louis Botha (an Afrikaner) as the first Prime Minister, never received the full support of the Afrikaners. Paul Kruger, an Afrikaner and former President of the Transvaal, committed himself to work for a unified nation, but J.B.M. Hertzog, another Afrikaner leader, continued to build a nationalism for an "oppressed people." Hertzog pledged himself to the overthrow of the victorious British, through formation of the National Party in 1912, and opposition to the "Allies" in World War I.

While the whites were fighting among themselves, the Africans began to use the new urban and industrial centers for development of their own organizational structures. The tribes, conquered and without arms, still maintained some social and judicial controls, especially in rural areas. But the tribe had no natural role in the developing industrial society.

In 1912 the African National Congress (ANC) was formed with its headquarters in Johannesburg. The first president, the Revd. John Dube, had studied in England, and members of the ANC were African men who had obtained an education mainly through English-run mission schools. Many of these members had also been sent abroad by the missions for further education and professional training. (At that time mission schools segregated students by sex and taught home-making skills to the girls.) Not surprisingly a number of the ANC leaders were clergy. The initial role of the ANC was to attempt to persuade the white power structure to recognize non-whites as equals.

The establishment of the formal Union of South Africa neces-sitated further development of political parties. The party structure, however, remained unset for several years. The parties with clear cut doctrine were the National Party, formally estab-lished in 1912; the Labor Party, established in 1908; the Communist Party, 1921; and the South African Party, 1920.

With industrialization came the formation of trade unions, mainly by white skilled craft workers who emigrated from England during the late 19th century. It was only with the development of industrial unions that a trade union movement was begun. But immediately the issues of racial integration and job protection/classification arose. Should non-whites be allowed to organize? Should they be allowed to obtain training and to hold skilled positions? Generally, the people who argued that the "worker," not race, is the common bond were labeled socialists, or communists. And the more the Government defined race as its major concern, and the more Africans moved into urban areas, the more the craft unions were anxious to deal with the Government and employers to segregate

3

jobs for whites and those for non-whites.

These various forces and organizations, jelled by industrial-ization, urbanization, and the Boer War, have interacted constantly throughout the sixty-eight years since formation of the Union of South Africa.

Each of the following chapters covers one decade and is broken into four parts:

1. an overview of the decade, covering legislation, major events, and social and economic developments;
2. anti-apartheid events;
3. the role of women in anti-apartheid organizations; and
4. individual women in the anti-apartheid movement.

The term anti-apartheid is construed broadly to include opposition to racial separation and/or discrimination. Included within this definition are black nationalist organizations who endorsed a policy of separatism as necessary to achieving equality. Also included are multi-racial trade unions and non-white trade unions, both of which opposed the exclusion of Africans from the definition of employee under the Industrial Conciliation Act, as amended. Because the Communist Party was the organization which most consis-tently followed a policy of equality and integration (except for the Black National Republic period of 1929-1931), and because the opposed all discriminatory and separatist legislation, Party Communists became the primary target of the Government. Then everyone who opposed apartheid and the white Government came under the threat of being labeled a communist.

The following review of the status of women in South Africa describes the context within which women took action against the Government's apartheid policy.

CHAPTER 2

II. STATUS OF WOMEN

Because South African society has so many rigid stratifications by race and economic group, the status of women is difficult to define except to say the women of any group are less than equal to the men. Since most South African laws apply to specific racial groups, the status of women must be reviewed by racial group.

During the celebration in 1971 of the tenth anniversary of the Republic of South Africa the National Union of South African Students (NUSAS) issued a leaflet which raises the basic issues in the lives of blacks in South Africa:

South Africa has
+ The highest per capita prison population in the world. Between July 1969 and June 1970, 2,016,300 cases were taken to court, 44 percent (932,127) of which involved technical offenses - influx control and curfew violations by Africans.
+ The highest rate of hangings in the Western world, and 50 percent of the total legal executions in the world.
+ One of the highest rates of violent crime.
+ The only country in the world to legalize the breaking up of marriages by the State because of racial laws.
+ One of the highest suicide rates and one of the highest death through malnutrition rates for comparable countries.
+ One of the greatest gaps between education expenditures for whites and for blacks.
+ One of the largest police forces per capita in the world.
+ The world record for quick court cases (20 seconds in the pass courts) and the world record for long detentions before and without trials.

Burdens in everyday living born by African, Indian, and Colored South Africans, which fall heavily upon women are:

Group Areas Act removals to Reserves/Homelands (geographical areas set aside for Africans of a particular tribal ancestry), usually with no preparation, no housing, no jobs, no facilities.

Influx control which can prohibit the wife from joining her husband in an urban area and can force her to leave an urban area upon divorce, illness, or widowhood.

5

Contract labor under which neither the husband
nor the wife can take the family to the urban
area when working by contract. (Until the seventies this generally applied only to men working
in the mines. Since then hostels have been built
for other male workers and for "single" women
workers.)

Requirement that women in the Reserves feed
Government work crews and fill dipping tanks,
without pay or reimbursement.

Lack of hospitals and medical care, schools, and
food in the Reserves.

The above items lay out the effects of some of the racial
legislation on the lives of black women. In addition the governmental, social, economic, and religious structures in South Africa
bear many of the same characteristics of subordination of women as
are characteristic of other countries. The resulting economic
status of African women is that out of a population of seven and a
half million African women 800,000 were classified in 1960 as
economically active:

50 percent as domestic servants,
25 percent as workers on white farms,
25,000 as professionals (including 12,000 nurses and
11,000 teachers),
and the remainder working in factories or as clerks.

Wages of these women workers have been estimated through
various studies. The average annual wages for Africans working
in private manufacturing were found by the South African Institute
of Race Relations in 1950, at which time 53 percent of the workers
were African, to be R258 ($361) for men and R246 ($344) for women.
(The wage differential between men and women was much smaller for
African than for other racial groups.) In general factory and
clerical workers averaged R226. The Financial Mail estimated in
1965 that 41 percent of all African workers received less than
R48.00 per month (R578 per year), the official poverty level.
African nurses in 1960 received an average of R800 ($1120); nursing
sisters, R1,000 ($1400), while white nursing sisters received
double that amount. In 1970 African men teachers were earning
R1260 - 2610 and African women with the same qualifications, R1140
- 2160.
In 1973 the Government proposed minimum wage levels for
unskilled workers which established wage differentials between men
and women of up to R 34.8 per year in the first year, with men
receiving up to R174; and a differential of up to R39.6 per year
in the second year, with men receiving up to R198. These wage
levels are excluded from coverage by the Unemployment Insurance
Act, and all fall below the official poverty level.
An analysis of monthly earnings of Africans in Bethal and

Viljoenskroon and their surrounding rural areas in 1972, conducted by the University of South Africa's Market Research Bureau, found the following:

Average Monthly Earnings

	food/mo. (in kind)	men	women	%unskilled
Bethal	R11.34	R24.12	R13.32	84
Viljoenskroon	10.65	19.63	10.93	87
Johannesburg	35.84	63.52	33.90	35

In the mid-seventies approximately 73 percent of African women were living in rural areas. Of the 27 percent living in urban areas, 80 percent were employed in domestic service. Most of these women earned less than R130 cash wages per year. (The Anglican Archbishop in 1973 urged payment of R79 monthly to living out domestics, and R54 monthly to those who live in, making an annual wage of R948 or R648.)

Under apartheid rules employers of domestic workers may provide a room, separate from the house, for the worker to stay in during the week. Apartment buildings usually reserve the top floor for rooms for domestic servants. If the women return to their own homes in the locations or townships, areas where Africans in urban areas are allowed to live separate from the white areas, they may have to travel for at least an hour each way, at a cost of approximately R2 per month. With the stress on contract labor in the seventies women domestic workers were no longer allowed to have their babies or very young children with them at work, and they still could not have their husbands or male friends visit or spend the night.

Of the 73 percent of the African women living in the rural areas or reserves, in the mid-seventies, only 13.6 percent of those able to work were employed in remunerative jobs. Rural women are less mobile than men, both because of their socially required responsibility for children and because if they leave a homestead, they lose the right to cultivate the family land.

Very few African women have recieved professional training. As of 1970 there were no African women attorneys, government administrators, engineers, architects, veterinarians, chemists, or university professors. Only 0.1 percent of all African women attend secondary school. Under the mission schools women were not encouraged, if even allowed, to obtain an academic education or skill training.

As of 1960 the following numbers of men and women in each racial group had passed Standard Ten or received a diploma or degree:

	Men	Women	Total Population
African	10,872	3,511	10,907,789
Colored	6,246	2,183	1,509,258

	Men	Women	Total Population
Asian	5,623	894	477,125
White	401,599	317,671	3,088,492

Under South African civil and tribal law women are not citizens in their own right. Their status usually is determined by the closest male relative - husband, brother, father, son. Only men can enter into contracts, hold property rights, or determine heritage. To marry, an African woman living in Natal, no matter her age, must have a male guardian's consent. A woman cannot automatically take over her husband's business if he is incapacitated or dies. She must apply for permission from the Government, which can be refused on the grounds the woman has no minors to support. Women's incomes, however, are taxed separately and irrespective of the number of dependents. And, if the man who is the woman's "guardian" defaults on payment of taxes, the woman is held responsible.

Single, divorced, and widowed women are in a particularly vulnerable position and subject to arbitrary "removals" by the Government:

> Women have absolutely no security unless their passes indicate that they are married to a man who is in lawful employment. When the husband loses his job then the whole family is in danger of deportation. On the other hand, if the woman finds it difficult to get on with her husband she cannot leave him, since she is subject to immediate removal from the area as a single woman. (Florence Mophosho, Sechaba, 8.70., vol. 4.8; p. 17)

The matrimonial Affairs Act of 1953 provided the first real security for African women by requiring that

> no husband may, without his wife's written consent, alienate or confer any real right in immovable property which belongs to his wife or which she brought into the community. Nor may any husband, without the wife's written consent, receive or take possession of any remuneration or dividends due to her, or of compensation awarded to her in respect of personal injuries she has sustained, or of any deposit standing in her name in a financial institution, or other amounts due to her personally from any other source. Any married woman may without assistance become a depositor in a savings institution. Should her husband desert her, she may obtain an order of court declaring any property subsequently acquired by her to be free of her husband's control. (Horrell, The Rights of African Women, pp. 10-11)

The black woman's reference book, however, required as of

1960, requires information on her male guardian or husband, whereas the man's reference book includes information only on him.

As part of the new push to implement apartheid, in 1972 the Government opened a hostel in the Alexandra location to house 2,834 single women, i.e. all women working under contract, separated from their families. All the doors are electronically operated from the gate, and can be locked to prohibit movement by residents. The facilities include one bath per 25 residents, one basin and one toilet per 20 residents, and one shower per 35 residents.

In 1973 the Government began to require the following language in contracts to be signed by women domestic workers living in urban areas:

> I..., the undersigned, hereby declare that the details furnished by me are correct and I fully understand that the service contract entered into will be cancelled forthwith if any of my children/ dependents join me in the prescribed area or if I fail to utilize the prescribed accommodation.

And the employer has to sign a similar document:

> I..., the undersigned, being the employer of the Bantu female..., accept it as a specific condition of her employment that she will not be allowed to introduce any of her children/dependents into the prescribed area and that the service contract will be terminated if she:
> (a) Introduces her children/dependents into the area; or
> (b) Fails to reside in approved accommodation whether it be on my own premises, hostel or any other housing.
> (Race Relations News, 11.73, p. 7)

In addition children who do grow up in the Reserves have no legal right to be with their parents in the urban areas when they turn 18. Many children of common law marriages who in the past were able to grow up in urban areas have no legal status because the "marriage" was never legal, and the mother and the children never legally lived in the township. As a result the children could not attend school, have none of the papers required to seek work, and so now have no place legally to go.

Associated with low income, limited education, lack of housing, and massive resettlement and removals is malnutrition and lack of medical care. Few hospitals exist for care of Africans, especially in the rural areas. With the vast resettlement and removal schemes which the Government has conducted during the past two decades, whatever stability and basic nutrition which may have existed has vanished. The Reserves cannot support the people living there, mainly women, children, and the elderly. Proper food is not available. Power, water, sanitation, and transportation facilities generally do not exist. Parents must find work outside the Reserves, usually as seasonal laborers on white farms.

Cosmas Desmond reports in The Discarded People that in 1968, 22,000 people left their homes in the Taung magisterial district alone to work on white farms outside the Reserve from May until July or August. The children left behind and the parents themselves experience a high rate of gross pellagra, beri-beri, and scurvy. Also prevalent at an increasing rate are tuberculosis and kwashiorkor. In the Kuruman Reserve diptheria breaks out every year, yet no immunization program has been implemented. The 100,000 people living in the Tswana homeland, a 9,000 square mile area, are served by one small hospital managed by the Anglican Church.

The National Nutrition Research Institute estimated the incidence of Protein-Calorie Malnutrition to be 65,000 per year. Another study concluded that 80 percent of all African school-going children in Pretoria suffered from malnutrition or under nutrition. In Sekhukhuniland researchers estimate 50 percent of all children born alive die before their fifth birthday. (cf SPRO-CAS, Some Implications of Inequality)

Colored and Asian women experience much of the same oppression as African women. They, too, are subject to the color bar in jobs and education, to resettlement, and to restrictions in movement. The impact is not quite as severe because there are no reserves and tribal homelands to which they are supposed to belong. In the scale of races in South Africa Indians and Coloreds are a step above Africans, and, being fewer in number, are better able to look out for each other, obtain better education, and receive higher incomes.

Racially, white women in South Africa are at the top of the ladder. But as women they are a long way from being equal to the men who run the government, industries, farms, and churches. Just as in most other nations South African women are not expected to need to work, to need to maintain themselves or their families, to want to have a profession, or to make decisions about their own lives.

The white women who do work have first choice in secretarial positions - the "color bar" for women. The schools prohibit married women from teaching. White women are teachers and nurses, just as are non-white women, but their rate of pay is much higher. Because of this pay differential, and the low rate for domestic servants, most professional white women employ domestics, even if for only one day per week, to do the cleaning, washing, and ironing. (So much a part of the social system is this use of domestic servants that the only place washing can be hung out in apartment buildings in white areas is the roof, which is the "African" area.)

Married white women in urban areas who are raising families, whether or not they are working, usually employ fulltime domestic servants. It is not uncommon for a family to have one servant to look after the children and a second to clean and cook.

Life for the non-professional or poor white woman is not so easy. Evan the wage of a secretary is barely enough to live on in an urban area. Whereas the English-speaking South African men tend to receive professional training, have a craft, or go into administration or business, until the sixties Afrikaner men in the main stayed on the farms and worked in the mines. As a result the opportunities for Afrikaner women were even more severely restricted than those for English-speaking women. The attitudes of the Dutch Reformed Church (DRC) toward women made Afrikaner women completely subject to men. Because of their lack of education and restricted movement, Afrikaner women needing to work to survive generally became factory workers. In the thirties and forties these workers lived in hostels very similar to those now being built in African townships.

Afrikaner women factory workers are being particularly hard hit by the Government's border industry policy which is to develop industries near the African Reserves to provide jobs for Africans who either voluntarily or by legal restriction are living in the Reserves. A large proportion of the factories built on the borders, with numerous financial incentives from the Government, are for industries which traditionally employed large numbers of Afrikaner and Colored women: clothing, textiles, and knitting and woolen mills. As a result the established clothing industry experienced a crisis at the end of 1965 when eight clothing factories in Johannesburg, one in Parys, and one in Kimberley closed. (Garment Worker, 5.11.65) At the time the vice-president of the Afrikaanse Handelsinstituut suggested the entire clothing industry become a border industry. (Garment Worker, 8.10.65) The border clothing factories were then reporting profit increases of 30 percent through use of cheaper labor than that provided by the Afrikaner, Colored, and African women who had obtained trade union strength through the Garment Workers' Union. The Industrial Conciliation agreements obtained by the GWU were not allowed to be applied to border industries.

Beginning in the 1970s more industrial positions became open to blacks and women, through the shortage of white male skilled workers.

Trade unions have played a key role in improving the status of women in South Africa, and in their role in the anti-apartheid movement. The Industrial Conciliation Act of 1924, passed by the Nationalist and Labor "Pact" Government, excluded African men from the definition of "employee," thus barring them from membership in registered, i.e. official and legal, trade unions. As a result unions in predominantly male industries had to be completely, or nearly, all white. When African male workers organized, they formed all black or all-African unions.

The early women trade union organizers, though predominantly white, organized African, Indian, Colored, and white women into multi-racial unions - particularly the Food and Canning Workers' Union, the Sweet Workers' Union, the Textile Workers' Union, the Garment Workers' Union. They knew that isolated by race they could have no bargaining power. White male organizers, on the other hand, willingly gave up trade union bargaining power for the industrial color bar - reservation of certain jobs for white men.

Since the thirties women trade union leaders of all races have fought the white male industrial, political, and religious power structure. The unions provided the training ground for most of the women leaders in the movement against apartheid and for an improved status for women. The women who did not come into the anti-apartheid movement via the unions were mainly white, and English-speaking.

In general women had no leadership role, in the economic, social, religious, or political structures in South Africa from formation of the Union in 1910 through 1975. Every established institution excluded women, or allowed only a few token representatives. From this perspective the role of women in the anti-apartheid movement takes on an aura of women separate from the power hierarchies, establishing their own place, and declaring their personhood separate from traditional institutions and organizations.

CHAPTER 3

III. THE TWENTIES

The first World War severely inhibited efforts by leaders of the new nation to develop a coherent process and working structure for policy-making and economic development. While the Union Government was officially at war against Germany, Afrikaner nationalists organized military units to oppose the Union and to assist the Germans in South West Africa. White and African workers staged numerous strikes, and the Government took a position hostile to all trade unions. In 1918 the Government began to formalize the separation of races in the workplace. The Factory Act required separate facilities - toilets, restrooms, and canteens - for each race.

The 1922 Rand strike by Afrikaner miners, which ended with the Government declaring martial law and dropping bombs on Benoni, brought together the Afrikaner nationalist and the Afrikaner miner who felt that the English-speaking mine-owners considered the Afridaner miner to be the same as the non-white miner. In fact they were competing for the same unskilled jobs. The newly formed Communist Party of South Africa (CPSA), members of which participated in the strike leadership, attempted to keep racism out of the strike, - an especially difficult task when the mines were hiring Africans as scabs - and to concentrate on the conditions and wages of all workers.

Following the strike and the end of martial law the Smuts Government was voted out, in 1923, and the National and Labor Parties' "Pact" Government, with General J.B.M. Hertzog as Prime Minister, was voted in. Their platform had been to establish the color bar, or job reservation by race in industry. To the Afrikaner worker the color bar was more important than organizing unions. Then, in 1929 the Afrikaner National Party gained its own majority in Parliament.

As part of the legislative package pressed by General Hertzog the Industrial Conciliation Act was passed in 1924, providing for the regulation and registration of trade unions and employers' organizations, the establishment of industrial councils consisting of representatives of trade unions and employers' associations, formation of boards, and appointment of arbitrators. African males were excluded from the definition of employee. A violation of an industrial council agreement, which, once approved by the Minister of Labor, had the force of law, was made a criminal offense. In 1925 the color bar became law under the Mines and Works Act, and the Wage Board legislation established the mechanism for labor negotiations in industries where employees and employers were not organized into registered organizations. The Wage Boards were intended to apply particularly to African male workers who had been excluded from coverage by the Industrial Conciliation Act (ICA). Then in the 1930 amendment to the ICA the principle of equal pay for equal work was extended to Africans who were employed in the same type of work as that covered by an industrial council agreement.

The 1923 Urban Areas Act instituted controls over the movement of Africans into urban areas, and in 1925 Afrikaans became the second official language.

Meanwhile in 1920 the First National Conference of Non-White Trade Unions had been held and the Industrial and Commercial Workers Union (ICWU) formed as a national federation of non-white trade unions. The ICWU decided to devote special attention to the organization of agricultural laborers and women workers. In 1921 the ICWU took a position condemning the farm labor system and the mine recruitment system. The killing in 1921 by white police of 163 members of the African millenarian sect, the Israwlites, at Bulhoek, further motivated African workers to organize.

In 1926 the South African Trade Union Congress (SATUC) was formed in an effort to coordinate all trade unions. Even though African unions could not be registered, and only whites were accepted as members of the SATUC, the official ploicy of the SATUC was to represent and unite all workers. Since many of the white unions supported the color bar, this ploicy simply prevented SATUC from taking antagonistic action toward non-white workers and organizations.

In 1928 the Non-European Trade Union Federation (NTUF), claiming 10,000 members in the Witwatersrand alone, was formed through the efforts of the Communist Party. African unions organized by Communist trade unionists in the 1920s covered the laundry, baking, clothing, mattress, and furniture industries. A total of 82 unions were formed.

1929 brought the founding of the South African Institute of Race Relations (SAIRR), the stated purpose of which was to collect and disseminate factual information, and of the Federasie van Afrikaanse Kultuurverenigings (F.A.K.) (Federation of Afrikaner Cultural Organizations), the purpose of which was to make the Afrikaner culture and language predominant in South Africa.

During the twenties both white and non-whites gradually moved into the urban areas. Mining and manufacturing industries expanded, with an increase in the number of mining employees from 309,000 in 1920 to 354,000 in 1927; and of manufacturing employees, from 175,000 in 1920 to 202,000 in 1927. The increase in the number of non-white mining and manufacturing workers during this period was 52,402.

A. Anti-Apartheid Events

Most of the "anti-apartheid" events during the 1920s convey an optimism that through the existing political and economic structures change could be achieved which would provide equality, justice, and freedom for all residents of South Africa. Some of the main anti-apartheid events were:

1918   Formation of the Industrial and Commercial Workers Union (ICWU).

1919	Women's anti-pass campaign.
1920s	Organizing of African and mixed trade unions.
1920	Rand Strike by 40,000 African miners.
1920	Strikes by ICWU in Port Elizabeth. Leader arrested, followed by protests during which 23 Africans were killed.
1920-1924	Anti-pass demonstrations by women.
1921-1929	Communist Party candidates ran for the Cape municipal council, the Durban town council, and for the seats to represent Cape "Natives" in Parliament.
1924	Protests against the "Hertzog Bills."
1925	Convention of African Chiefs to protest discriminatory laws as being contrary to the African legal system.
1927	Founding of the Joint Councils of Europeans and Natives.
1928	Non-European Trade Union Federation formed by unions not allowed in the South African Trade Union Congress.
1929	Women's anti-pass campaign in the Orange Free State.
1929	Founding of the South African Institute of Race Relations.
1929	Formation of the League of African Rights to extend the franchise to all Africans, to achieve universal free education, to abolish the pass laws, and to gain freedom of speech and association for all. (Several branches in the Transkei.)
1929	Collapse of the ICWU following expulsion of the communists, including several leaders, in 1926.

B. The Role of Women in Anti-Apartheid Organizations Trade Unions

Organizing non-white workers into trade unions and forming multi-racial unions was de-facto anti-apartheid. In the organizing of trade unions in the twenties women played minor roles except in the clothing industry and waitressing. The Trade Union Congress and the Industrial and Commercial Workers' Union did not involve women in their leadership.

The initial trade union organizing by industry developed in the twenties by the ICWU, the CPSA, and SATUC included women workers. One of the earliest of such unions was the Witwatersrand Tailors' Association, a white union, consisting of and organized by women. The Native Clothing Workers' Union also consisted mainly of women members, all African. Although women (400 white and 120 black) united in strike in 1928 to save the jobs of three white women trade union organizers, the African workers did not receive the same support when they struck. The Waitresses Industrial Council, established under the ICA, suffered organized terrorism in 1927.

Political Parties. Only the Communist Party actively opposed racial segregation and inequality in the twenties. The CPSA had two women members on the Central Executive Committee. Both campaigned, but for their husbands (women could not vote nor hold public office) and both participated as speakers at public meetings. The CPSA was actively involved in organizing non-white trade unions, including women workers, and in establishing night schools for workers and training programs for union and Party organizers, male and female.

Women played an important role in the campaign sponsored by the League of African Rights to obtain one million signatures to the Petition of Rights.

Non-White Nationalist Organizations. The African National Congress, organized in 1912, was the main nationalist organization opposed to apartheid in the twenties. In 1920 the ANC refused to participate in the organizing conference of the ICWU, but the organizer and head of the women's section of the ANC did attend and did urge the organizing of African workers, including women. The ANC did not accept women as full members and so did not make women an integral part of the organization. However, the women organized and led the anti-pass campaigns of the twenties which opposed extension of the pass to women.

Interracial Organizations. The South African Institute of Race Relations was formed only in 1929, with no women as officers. The predecessor to the Institute, the Joint Councils of Europeans and Natives, had few women members.

C. Individual Women in the Anti-Apartheid Movement

Prior to 1920 women active in the effort to attain equal rights for women and for non-whites included Olive Emily Schreiner, Julia Frances Solly, Rebecca Notlowitz (who married S.P. Bunting in 1916), Mary Fitzgerald, Laurie Green, and Charlotte Maxeke. The first two fought for the vote for women in the 1890s and early 1900s and served as leaders of the National Council of Women. In 1911 both Olive Schreiner and J.F. Solly attended the Universal Races Congress in London, a report on which prepared by Ms Solly was published in the South Africa Journal of Science in 1911. Ms. Schreiner became well known for her novels, and for her statement in Closer Union (1909) urging freedom and opportunity, just and humane treatment, for men and women of all races. The writer, Nathaniel Weyl, refers to Ms. Schreiner as by 1917 having become "a zealous Communist." (Traitors' End, p. 47) Ms. Schreiner's husband changed his name to hers when they married.

Rebecca Notlowitz, Mary Fitzgerald, and Laurie Green were active in various socialist organizations prior to 1920, and Rebecca Notlowitz Bunting became a founding member of the CPSA in 1921.

Mary Fitzgerald was active in the Johannesburg area in the decade between 1910 and 1920, especially on behalf of miners and women workers. She along with Dora Montefiore and three men were instrumental in forming the United Socialist Party in 1912, open to any socialist of any color, race, creed, or sex. Ms. Fitzgerald and Archie Crawford, her husband, printed the USP publications, and actively participated in the leadership of the 1912 miners' strike, calling for a general strike on July 4. When the miners' agreement with the Government was signed, they opposed it as a "bluff." In July 1921 Mary Fitzgerald led the attack of the Women's Industrial League on the French Club in Johannesburg, demanding the replacement of Colored waiters with white waitresses. This action symbolizes the end of her involvement in the "anti-apartheid" movement.

Laurie Green ran for Parliament in 1910 as a socialist candidate representing Pietermaritzburg. She actively recruited Africans into socialist organizations, including preparing and distributing publications in African languages. In 1919 she co-authored a pamphlet, "Workers of South Africa," published in Zulu and Sotho, calling on workers of all races to revolt, for which she was arrested. In the 1920s Ms. Green actively participated in the Industrial and Commercial Workers Union, headed by Clement Kadalie, and according to the Simons she was probably the only white member of the ICU in Natal. (Simons, The Color Bar, p. 364)

When Clement Kadalie first began to organize the African ICWU as a means to combat the inequalities and deprivations of African workers, he received the support of Charlotte Manye Maxeke, head of the ANC Bantu Women's League, for the initial Conference of Non-White Trade Unions held in 1920. Ms. Maxeke had already had a long history of organizing anti-pass demonstrations, having in 1913 successfully forced the government of the Orange Free State (the only province then requiring women to carry a pass) to abandon the effort to extend passes to women. This was achieved only after mass demonstrations, arrests, and imprisonment of women, and after Ms. Maxeke had led a delegation to meet with Prime Minister Botha.

Ms. Maxeke had organized the women's section of the African National Congress earlier in 1913 after having been one of the original founders of the ANC itself. In 1908 she founded, jointly with her husband, the first college for Africans in the Transvaal, Wilberforce Institute at Evaton near Pietermaritzburg, named after Wilberforce University in Ohio from which she had obtained a Bachelor of Arts degree in 1905.

In the first half of the twenties Ms. Maxeke led demonstrations in Johannesburg, and Ms. T. Mapikela led similar demonstrations in the Orange Free State, against renewed Government efforts to extend the pass to women, the result of these mass demonstrations by women was in some cases withdrawal of the pass laws for women, and in many others, relaxation of the laws. During demonstrations the women dumped bags of passes at municipal offices. Ms. Maxeke also campaigned to have women replace men as domestic workers, and she opened an employment office for women. In the mid-twenties she became a probation officer in Johannesburg. Mary Benson in Struggle for a Birthright lists Charlotte Maxeke as one of the three "main leaders" of the ANC in the twenties.

The Communist Party in the twenties was very small. The only references found of women active in the Party were of Jessie Mpama, an African woman from Potchefstroom, Rebecca Notlowitz Bunting, and Mary Zelikowitz Wolton. Rebecca Bunting served on the Central Executive Committee beginning in 1921, the only woman out of 14 members. During the 1922 miners' strike Rebecca Bunting supported the miners but tried, unsuccessfully, to keep race from being an issue. She was instrumental in the Communist Party adopting the position in 1924 that being a communist meant being openly identified with the emancipation of all non-white people.

Sidney Percival Bunting (General Secretary of the Party) and Douglas Wolton ran in 1929 as Communist Party candidates for the Native Representative seats in Parliament for Tembuland (Transkei) and the Cape Flats respectively. Rebecca Bunting and Molly Wolton actively campaigned with their husbands in the Reserves. Both were arrested several times and were followed by the Security Branch police. The Buntings - and Gana Makabeni who was campaigning with them - were charged under the Riotous Assemblies Act. The Government, besides having the candidates followed, confiscated publications and leaflets, and threatened people who attended meetings. Eventually the Buntings won their case on appeal to the Supreme Court. Both Bunting and Wolton lost the election.

In 1929 Rebecca and Sidney Bunting were instrumental in establishing the League of African Rights, in conjunction with Josiah Gumede, President of the ANC. The League distributed a Petition of Rights calling for the end of the pass laws, universal education, franchise for Africans in all provinces, and freedom of speech and association for people of all races. Several branches were organized in the Transkei where the Buntings had been campaigning. But in the Dingaan's Day (December 16) demonstrations held in that same year only the League of African Rights, the Communist Party, (CP) and the ICU (formerly the ICWU) participated. In Potchefstroom whites entered the township to break up the demonstration and fired shots at a CP leader, Edwin Mofutsanyana (General Secretary of the CP in the thirties), which killed another CP member. Josie Mpama (later married to Mofutsanyana), Rebecca Bunting, and two male leaders of the CP, called a protest meeting in Potchefstroom and encouraged African residents in the township to overcome their fears and to oppose the attacks of the white racists.

The Communist International (CI) decided in 1930 the League of African Rights was not correct communist policy, and, with Rebecca Bunting openly opposing the new CI position endorsing Black Nationalism, Molly and Douglas Wolton and Lazar Bach took over control of the Communist Party. Molly Wolton is reported to have been an effective, fiery speaker. She was particularly active in organizing the unemployed of all races and in holding interracial marches. In 1932 Molly Wolton was banished under the Riotous Assemblies Act, and shortly thereafter the Woltons returned to England.

During the time the Woltons ran the CP, the trade union activists in the Party who urged development of multiracial unions and establishment of a unified working class were expelled from the Party. (During those years the CI endorsed Black Nationalism, the formation of a Native Republic.) Of the six leaders expelled, only one - Fanny Klenerman Glass - was a woman.

In 1929 Edith and J.D. Rheinallt Jones developed the Joint Councils of Europeans and Natives, the precursor to the South African Institute of Race Relations. Edith Rheinallt Jones, Winnifred Hoernlé (both later very active in the SAIRR), and Charlotte Maxeke were the only women members on the first Council in Johannesburg, out of 37 white and 37 "Native" members. The Councils, consisting of local people, were to improve local

18

conditions for non-whites and to initiate community action. The SAIRR took on the task of organizing the Councils upon its formation in 1929.

Edith Rheinallt Jones led much of the opposition to the Color Bar Bill of 1925, accusing the Chamber of Mines of financing efforts to keep wages down. Ruth Fry was the only woman of six signators to an appeal for funds in 1925 to fight the "Hertzog Bills", which included the Color Bar Bill.

In 1929 the National Party took over the Government and launched a campaign against the opposition to white supremacy. In December of that year Olive Schreiner participated in a deputation from the ANC, ICU, and white "liberals" to the Minister of Native Affairs, seeking complete repeal of the pass laws. They failed.

In the 1920s can be seen the bases from which women would develop their direction and their strength in the anti-apartheid movement. In the twenties women generally played secondary roles in the trade union organizations, the Communist Party, the African National Congress, and the South African Institute of Race Relations. And these were the only structures making any effort to achieve equality and freedom of speech and association. Only when the women went on their own, such as in the pass demonstrations, were they recognized as leaders. The women's victory in prohibiting the extension of the pass to women was the only success of the anti-apartheid movement in the 1920s except for the early formation of a few multiracial unions, which included women workers and were organized by women trade unionists.

CHAPTER 4

IV. THE THIRTIES

With the election of the National Party in 1929 the direction of the South African Government was even more clearly set toward domination by the Afrikaner Nationalists. By 1937 the F.A.K., the Federation of Afrikaner Cultural Organizations, had 300 Afrikaner organizations as affiliates and had established itself as the sole authority to set social, economic, and political policy for Afrikaners.

Essential to Afrikaner Nationalist control in South Africa was for all Afrikaners to be brought under Nationalist domination. The only predominantly Afrikaner organizations which held any independent power were the trade unions, in particular the Mine Workers Union and the Garment Workers Union. During the thirties the F.A.K. made every effort to place its people in leadership positions in these unions and to instigate a breaking away of Afrikaner members from any "mixed" unions. In 1939 the White Workers' Protection Society was formed to oppose the existing multi-racial trade unions.

This Nationalist effort took on all the characteristics of the national socialists of the time in Europe. In South Africa the violence was conducted by the "Grey Shirts." Their efforts were quite successful, except with the GWU, and included the murder in 1939 of the head of the white Mine Workers Union, Charles Harris, who would not bow to Nationalist pressure.

The thirties brought legislation limiting the rights of non-whites to own land, to move, to assemble. Some of this legislation also served to control whites who did not support Government policy.

The Riotous Assemblies Act passed in 1930, an extension of the 1914 Act, gave the Government the power to prohibit any assembly which caused friction among the races, or which might endanger the public peace. The Act was used to prohibit gatherings which criticized Government policy and existing laws.

The Natives (Urban Areas) Amendment Act (1930), the Native Land and Trust Act (1936), and the Native Land and Trust Amendment Act (1939) expanded the efforts incorporated into the Natives' Land Act of 1913 to prevent non-whites, especially Africans, from becoming an integral part of South African society. Thirteen and seven-tenths percent of the land in South Africa was set aside for Africans. Although Africans would be allowed to live in certain other designated areas, they could never be land-owners or permanent residents. And they could live in those areas only with the consent of the Government.

The Native Representation Act of 1936 removed all franchised Africans (certain qualified men living in the Cape Province) from the common voting rolls. Those Africans were given three seats in the House of Assembly, but their representatives had to be white. This representation lasted from 1937 to 1960, when the seats were abolished.   In addition the Act made provisions for Africans living throughout the country to elect four white Senators and for creation of a Natives' Representative Council, to be organized under the executive branch of the Government, chaired by the Secretary for Native Affairs, and having five white and four African members appointed by the Government and twelve Africans elected by the people. (This Council was abolished in 1951.)

The Government had extended the vote to white women in 1930, which halved the impact of the Cape Colored vote in the Cape Province, since Colored women still could not vote, and Cape Colored males were the only non-whites (after 1936) still on the common voting roll. This Act was perceived by non-whites as an additional effort to reduce their participation in the Government.

In 1934 Smuts' South African Party joined Hertzog's National Party to form the United Party. Dr. D.F. Malan then split from the National Party. (Malan was an active member of the F.A.K.) The number of persons voting doubled in the 1938 election, in which the "pure" nationalists (Malan) received 259,500 votes and the United Party, 446,000. The Labor Party reached its peak in that election, receiving 48,600 votes. Then in 1939 the United Party split over the vote to declare war on Germany, and Hertzog's nationalists voted with the Malan nationists against the declaration, losing by only seven votes. Hertzog served as Prime Minister throughout the thirties, but Smuts resumed the position after the war vote in 1939.

Despite the worldwide financial problems of the 1930s the number of workers and the population in South Africa continued to increase. Between 1921 and 1936 the non-white population increased by 2,000,000 or 40 percent and the white, by 500,000, 33 percent. During that same period the percent of Africans living in urban areas increased from 12 to 17; and the percent of whites, from 56 to 65. The percent of national income coming from manufacturing increased from 13.2 in 1928 to 17.6 in 1938.

In the thirties registered trade union membership increased from 101,888 in 1931 to 189,000 in 1936, still a small fraction of the total work force. The number of strikes in the 1930s was three-fifths the number in the 1920s and involved vewer workers than did the strikes between 1928 and 1930. Restrictive legislation and economic strains may have had some causal effect on the reduction in strikes, but the use of negotiation by industrial unions to achieve legal agreements, as provided in industrial conciliation legislation, eased many labor tensions.

In 1930 the South African Trade Union Congress disbanded and the South African Trades and Labor Council (SAT&LC) was formed. The SAT&LC adopted a policy of allowing non-white unions to affiliate. In 1937 the SAT&LC claimed 38 affiliated unions, 2 non-white. In 1939 the Council recommended to the Government that African trade unions be recognized, i.e. allowed to register, and so to negotiate and to strike. The Non-European Trade Union Federation continued to function throughout the 1930s, despite the change in the SAT&LC's policy.

A. Anti-Apartheid Events

1930s   Organizing of African, Colored, and multi-racial unions.
1930s   Members of the Communist Party elected to several munici-
              pal councils.
1930   Anti-Pass Campaign. Pass burning on Dingaans Day
              (December 16). Nkosi, head of the Durban branch of
              the CP and ANC leader, killed when the police moved
              in.
1930   Demonstrations against the Riotous Assemblies Act.
1930   SAT&LC formed, including non-white members.
9.1931   National Conference of Women.
3.1932   Germiston Women's demonstration against pass laws and
              evictions.
1932   GWU General Strike.
1933   African People's Convention.
1935   All-African Convention formed to organize opposition
              to the Hertzog bills.
1937   First Natives' Representatives (all white) elected to
              Parliament, all anti-apartheid.
1937   National Liberation League formed in Cape Town.
1938   Non-European United Front formed.

B.   The Role of Women in Anti-Apartheid
Organizations Trade Unions

   The thirties was a vital decade for organizing women into
trade unions and for training women trade union organizers and
leaders. Much of the organizing took place under the direction
of the SAT&LC, but was performed by persons committed to the unity
of the working class, including workers of all races, and opposed
to the efforts of the Government to limit the freedom of workers,
hence of people of all races. Women organized the food and canning
workers, sweets workers, laundry workers, sugar cane workers,
tobacco workers, and garment workers. Many of these women trade
union leaders were also elected to the National Executive Committee
of the SAT&LC. Women trade unionists were in the forefront of the
opposition to the Afrikaner nationalists and to apartheid in the
unions.
   Political Parties. Between 1929 and 1932 the Communist Party
became somewhat disfunctional through interference by the Communist
International, change in policy from integration to Black Nationalism, and purging of leaders who had coordinated activities and
programs with other anti-apartheid organizations and had been
involved in trade union organizing. Without the technical assistance and leadership from these members of the CP, a few of whom
were women, the League of African Rights and the NTUF lost their
momentum. One of the three people who took over control of the
Party was a woman. By 1935, however, the Party was back under the
leadership of the expelled leaders.
   Despite the power struggle within the CP and the moves to
expel the integrationist trade unionists, labeled "reformers," the
CP organized a large anti-pass demonstration on Dingaan's Day,

December 16, in 1930. The result was the burning of 150 passes in Johannesburg, 400 in Pretoria, 300 in Potchefstroom, and 3,000 in Durban; and the murder of the head of the Durban branch of the CP, Johannes Nkosi, by the police. Though only men then carried passes, women of the CP conducted much of the organizing.

In the fall of 1931 the CP held a National Conference of Women and in March of 1932 organized a demonstration of women from the Germiston location. During the 1930s the Government conducted a campaign to arrest, banish, and deport all Communist Party leaders and to ban CP meetings. Women and men, white and non-white, suffered from this.

The Labor Party had a few women on its Executive Committee in the thirties, mainly politically active women trade unionists.

Non-White Nationalist Organizations. Under the 1936 Natives' Representation Act the Natives' Representative Council was formed by the Government, and all the members were men. In 1937, 1938, and 1939 the Council demanded abolition of the Pass Laws, and in 1937 also demanded that the Government remove the restrictions on influx, i.e. freedom of movement of Africans.

The National Liberation League, formed in 1937 and including the ANC, anti-apartheid church leaders - especially the Revd. Z.R. Mahabane, also of the ANC - leaders of non-white trade unions and of the CP, and the Non-European United Front (founded in 1938) continued the efforts of the late twenties to coordinate opposition to apartheid. A Colored woman from Cape Town, who was also a member of the Cape Town Municipal Council, served as president of both the National Liberation League and the Non-European United Front.

The ANC continued to make representations to the Government to abolish the pass laws, influx control, and other legislation limiting the rights of Africans, and the President served on the Natives' Representative Council. The ANC also participated in some anti-pass campaigns and in demonstrations against the Hertzog Bills. Women still had no integral role in the organization.

Interracial Organizations. During the thirties the SAIRR had a position titled Honorary Organizer of the Women's Section which was held continuously by a woman who also sat on the SAIRR Executive Committee. During the thirties two other women also sat on the Executive Committee, which had a total of 32 members. The number of Joint Councils of Europeans and Natives increased, but few women were appointed as members.

C. Individual Women in the Anti-Apartheid Movement

Molly Wolton, one of the three leaders of the Communist Party in the early thirties, organized the Unemployment Workers Union in 1931, and held meetings and multiracial marches and demonstrations throughout 1931 and 1932. During the March 1932 women's demonstration, organized by the CP and held outside the Germiston location, Molly Wolton was arrested while addressing the women, despite the efforts of the African women to protect her and the other speakers. At the demonstration Ms. Wolton and the Germiston location women demanded abolition of all pass laws for men and women, equal pay for equal work in factories and on farms, free medical attention for

women workers in factories and on farms, a milk allowance for
children, a 7-hour work day for women, abolition of the special
lodger's tax, free education for Native children, free meals and
books, an end to corporal punishment of children, secular education,
an end to police raids on Native women, abolition of fines and
extortions imposed on Native women for brewing beer, provision for
children of women prisoners, and the right for African miners'
wives to reside wherever they like. (Umschenz: February 19, 1932)
Following her trial Molly Wolton was banished under the provisions
of the Riotous Assemblies Act. Then in 1933 her husband, Douglas
Wolton, and Ray Alexander (trade union organizer) were sentenced
to three months hard labor and one month suspended sentence respectively on the charge of inciting bus and tram workers to strike.
Following Mr. Wolton's release from prison the couple returned to
England.

Perhaps the most important woman leader in the anti-apartheid
movement in the thirties was Zainunissa (Cissie) Gool, daughter of
Dr. Abdurahman, a leader in the Cape Colored community. In 1931
Ms. Gool spoke at a Cape Town rally opposing the legislation which
gave white women, but not Colored, Indian, and African women, the
vote. In 1937 after the trade unionists and integrationists had
reemerged in the Communist Party leadership in South Africa, the
National Liberation League was formed with the slogan "Equality,
Land, and Freedom" and Cissie Gool was elected the first president.
She also became the first president of the Non-European United
Front, founded in 1938, which demanded repeal of racial laws. Ms.
Gool stated the NEUF's "'weapons will be the strike, the boycott
and peaceful demonstrations.'" (Simons, 502) Her father refused
to join the NEUF. He had, however, supported his daughter's
successful campaign for a seat on the Cape Town Municipal Council.
In addition Ms. Gool had been elected one of the two women members,
out of a total of six members, of the reformed Political Bureau of
the CP. The headquarters of the CP were moved at that time to
Cape Town in an effort to reduce the political infighting.

Other women in the Abdurahman/Gool family active in Colored
opposition to apartheid were Nellie Abdurahman, Cissie Gool's
mother; Dr. Waradia Abdurahman, Cissie Gool's sister; and Cissie
Gool's two sisters-in-law, Minnie and Janub Gool. In 1935 Minnie
Gool was sentenced to one month in prison for distributing an anti-
imperialist pamphlet during the celebration of 25 years of George
V's reign.

One of the four leaders of the National Liberation League who
opposed whites holding office in the League was Ms. Hawa Ahmed.
The four tried to hold a coup in 1939 but failed. A white Trotskyist
group which supported the attempted coup included a former nun, Ms.
C.R. Goodlatte. When the coup failed, Ms. Goodlatte apologized for
her involvement.

Josie Mpama, the first African woman leader in the CP, took a
leading role in urging Afridans to participate in the NEUF, along
with Indians and Coloreds. The Transvaal ANC refused to participate. In 1944 Ms. Mpama was elected a trustee of the National
Anti-Pass Council, organized to coordinate mass action through a
network of local anti-pass committees.

Rebecca Bunting continued to be active in CP activities in the thirties, including organizing demonstrations, distributing literature, and aiding victims of Government actions.

In the thirties several women began long careers in the trade union movement in South Africa:

Johanna Cornelius
Hestor Cornelius (Johanna's younger sister)
Bettie du Toit
Joey Fourie
Ray Alexander
Anna Scheepers

In the thirties du Toit, Alexander, and Fourie organized workers on the Cape: du Toit, Colored and Afrikaner women garment workers; Alexander, non-European railway and harbor workers, oat-meal workers, commercial employees, chemical workers, sweet workers, and laundry workers; Fourie, waitresses. (Du Toit and Fourie shared an attic apartment they called the "Oven" where they ate meals frequently consisting of raw vegetables which cost only three pence per pound.) These women organizers stressed the need for workers in an industry to be in one union, not to be broken up by craft, nor by race. They opposed the disunity which occurred in the 1928 strike when the white women did not support the African women workers, and they consistently urged elimination of the color bar in skilled trades, extension of training to all races, and free compulsory education for children of all races. None of these women organizers received a living wage for their work. They had to live in poverty and work long hours to organize workers who had no experience with trade unions.

In 1932 Johanna Cornelius organized the first general strike of garment workers against wage cuts. During the strike an Afrikaner woman worker was ridden down by the mounted police. In 1933 Ray Alexander was arrested and convicted along with Douglas Wolton under the Riotous Assemblies Act for inciting the tram and bus workers to strike. Then in a 1935 strike of garment workers in Industria, near Johannesburg, Johanna Cornelius and du Toit, along with three other women workers, were arrested and convicted under the same Act, being sentenced to 7 days hard labor. In prison they found themselves to be the only white women there who had not been arrested for prostitution.

In 1934 Johanna Cornelius was sent as a workers' delegate to the Soviet Union, following which she gave talks on how a better world for women workers and workers in general could be won. Ms. Cornelius was elected president of the GWU in 1935, and was succeeded by Anna Elizabeth Scheepers in 1937. (E.S. Sachs, one of the members of the CP expelled in 1931, was General Secretary.)

The Afrikaner women in the GWU were of special concern to the Afrikaner Nationalists, and the subject of numerous takeover attempts. The women consistently fought back, throwing the Nationalists out of meetings and defending themselves against physical attacks and beatings. Several women were injured during the thirties by the Nationalists, one at the hands of a Dutch

Reformed Church (DRC) predicant. (The Nationalists held Sachs, the only male involved in the leadership of the union, responsible for the women being in a multi-racial union and opposing Nationalist control.)

Johanna Cornelius called the attacks on the Afrikaner trade unions by the F.A.K. "a plot of capitalists and employers...to keep workers backward by fomenting race hatred." (Simons, p. 522)

Ray Alexander was elected, along with Cissie Gool, to the Political Bureau of the CP in 1938, and Johanna Cornelius to the Executive Committee of the Labor Party. Many of the women union organizers served on the National Executive of the SAT&LC, including J. Cornelius, du Toit, and Scheepers.

With the passage of the Natives' Representation Act providing for three white "Native Representatives," Margaret Ballinger ran as representative for Africans in Cape Eastern in 1937, and won. She had been a lecturer in history at the University of the Witwatersrand and an active member of the Johannesburg Joint Council of Europeans and Natives, formed in 1927. She and the other two Natives' Representatives in Parliament were not aligned with either the National or the United Party. In 1939 she cast a key vote to commit South Africa to the war against Hitler, a vote opposed by all Afrikaner nationalists. Ms. Ballinger served as Natives' Representative until 1960 when the seats were abolished.

Dr. Mabel Palmer, a Fabian socialist, ran multi-racial classes during the thirties at Sastri College in Durban, at which she lectured on socialism and Marxism. Several later anti-apartheid leaders studied with her. Both Dr. Palmer and Etheldra Lewis, another socialist teacher, are thought to have influenced their students by their endorsement of African trade unionism in the twenties and thirties.

Dr. Nellie Spilhaus, a member of the Executive Committee of the SAIRR during the 1930s, served as the first woman member of the Cape Provincial Council, from 1932-1942; President of the National Council of Women; and chair of the Cape School Board. Throughout these activities she opposed apartheid and worked to improve conditions and increase opportunities for non-whites.

Edith Rheinallt Jones served as the Honorary Organizer of the Women's Section of the SAIRR throughout the thirties, and as the only active organizer for the Institute. She also testified on behalf of the Institute against the Hertzog Bills in 1935.

In the thirties women again formed their own organizations and actions - unions, strikes, election to public office, demonstrations against the pass and other apartheid legislation. Women had secondary official roles within the recognized anti-apartheid organizations, except in the multi-racial unions and in the Communist Party. These exceptions include Zainunissa Gool's election as president of the National Liberation League and of the NEUF; her and Ray Alexander's election to the reformed Political Bureau of the CP; and the election of several women as officers and general secretaries of multi-racial unions. The women appear to have had little impact in the thirties. But it is possible that it was only through their strength and determination that the multi-racial unions survived the onslaught of the Nationalists. Their leadership in the unions and in the coalition efforts to oppose apartheid legislation and Government actions at least kept the anti-apartheid movement alive.

CHAPTER 5

V. THE FORTIES

Despite the narrow vote for entry of South Africa into World War II against the Germans, the Government under Smuts made a major commitment to the war effort. Blacks participated both in production of war materials and as members of the Native Military Corps (122,254), for which they expected a "return," but instead they continued to be on the receiving end of more and more restrictive legislation and administrative proclamations:

1941 Factory, Machinery and Building Works Act, providing for different regulations for different racial groups, covering accommodations and facilities.

1942 War Measure No. 145, prohibiting strikes by Africans.

1943 Native Administration Amendment Act, establishing an Advisory Council on Colored Affairs (abolished in 1950).

1944 Amendment to the 1922 Apprenticeship Act, precluding non-whites from participating in training and apprenticeship programs.

1945 Native Urban Areas Consolidation Act.

1945 Native Education Finance Act, based on taxation of Africans.

1945 Native Urban Areas Amendment Act.

1946 Asiatic Land Tenure and Indian Representation Act, limiting ownership and rental of property by Asians and providing for limited representation. (Latter portion repealed in 1948.)

1946 Riotous Assemblies Act, further limiting freedom of assembly.

1947 Industrial Conciliation (Natives) Act.

1948 Unemployment Insurance Amendment Act, excluding the majority of African Workers from unemployment benefits.

1949 Prohibition of Mixed Marriages Act.

1949 Native Laws Amendment Act, establishing labor bureaus to control influx of Africans into urban areas.

1949 Housing Amendment Act.

The legislation continued the direction set in the thirties: Indians were taken off the common voter rolls (1946), but were given no seats in Parliament; an Indian Representative Council was established, similar to the Natives' Representative Council set up in 1937; and Indian land rights were restricted to specific areas.

The Native Urban Areas Amendment Act culminated a long series of legislative efforts to control the movement of Africans into the urban, or "white," areas. Various land control Acts set aside 13.7 percent of the geographical area of South Africa for the "Natives," and the rest for whites. Despite these Acts Africans continued to work in the urban areas and to be recruited by white employers. The Government had to come up with a way to limit the number of Africans in the white areas but at the same time provide enough cheap labor for constantly expanding mining and manufacturing industries. Their solution was to control the "influx" of Africans by use of pass books and setting requirements for employment, length of residency, and family status. An African could remain in a "white" area only by permission of the Government, and the Government took sole authority for determining who would receive this permission.

In 1942 African workers staged a series of strikes for increased wages. Having no means of negotiating wages or working conditions under the Industrial Conciliation Act (ICA), African male workers had no alternative method to improve their situation. The war had increased the industrialization process, the number of jobs in manufacturing, and the types of jobs open to Africans. Employers, as well as most white workers, still viewed Africans as a source of cheap unskilled labor. The response of the Government to the strikes was War Measure 145 which prohibited African workers from striking. Nevertheless the number of strikes by African male workers continued to increase.

In 1946 the five-year-old African Mineworkers Union went out on strike. The average cash earnings of an African mineworker in 1946 was R7.2 ($10) per month, R0.23 ($0.32) per day. The AMWU voted in April to demand a minimum wage of R1 ($1.40) per day. Neither the employers nor the Government would respond to or meet with the union representatives. The union voted to go on strike on August 12th, and on the 13th the Cape Times reported 45,000 to 50,000 (out of 308,000) African mineworkers were on strike.

The Government responded with force: driving workers into the mines at bayonet point; baton charging groups of strikers who tried to walk to Johannesburg to demand to meet with Government representatives; sealing off the workers' living quarters; raiding the union offices; seizing documents, records, and membership lists; and arresting the union president, J.B. Marks, a member of the Communist Party. Through these actions the strike was broken.

The SAT&LC had an internal battle over whether or not to support the Government's action. In 1943 the Council had voted to back the AMWU's right to organize. Eventually those opposed to the Government's crushing of the strike and refusal to recognize the union won, but the SAT&LC could be of no assistance to the AMWU.

In 1946, and then again in 1947, the entire national Executive Committee of the Communist Party was arrested and charged with inciting the mineworkers to strike. The Supreme Court dismissed all the charges. Then the Parliament passed the 1946 amendments to the Riotous Assemblies Act prohibiting gatherings of more than 20 persons on mine property, and providing for banishment of any person thought guilty of fomenting hostility between races.

The Natives' Representative Council responded to the Government's refusal to recognize and negotiate with the AMWU by voting to conduct no business until the Government recognized African trade unions and began to deal with the injustices suffered by Africans. The Council was allowed to die.

In 1949 riots broke out in Durban with Zulus attacking Indians: 142 Indians were killed, 1,087 injured.

As a result of the continued divisions within the trade union movement over color and nationalism, the SAT&LC in 1941 represented only 21,500 workers, only 400 of whom were black. This membership included 46 affiliated unions, 8 of which were multi-racial or black. In 1947 the SAT&LC claimed to have 3 union affiliates with 184,041 members. In 1942, 29 African unions had formed the Council of Non-European Trade Unions, which by 1945 claimed to represent 119 unions with a total of 158,000 members. In 1949 the Afrikaner Nationalist movement formed the Coordinating Council of South African Trade Unions representing 13,000 white workers, including the South African Iron and Steel Trades' Association of the Government-owned ISCOR.

During the forties the Afrikaner Nationalists continued to take over white unions and other "cultural" organizations, and in 1948 with a campaign to achieve full, official apartheid, won 70 seats in Parliament with 402,000 votes. In coalition with the Afrikaner Party which won nine seats (42,000 votes) Dr. D.F. Malan formed the new Nationalist Government. The victory was won with an increase of only 80,000 votes over the 1943 election, while the United Party had gained an increase of 89,000 votes (a total of 524,000 votes) giving them 122,000 more votes than the victorious Nationalists, but only 63 seats.

South Africa's Gross Domestic Product (GDP) doubled in the forties and by 1949, 22.4 percent of the total national income came from manufacturing. The forties also brought a continuing increase in the number of blacks living in urban areas. By 1946, 22 percent of the Africans in South Africa (1,856,028) were living in urban areas, as compared with 17 percent (1,245,682) a decade earlier. And the total African population had increased 1.3 million. Thus by 1946 almost 100,000 more Africans than whites lived in the urban areas.

In 1946 the majority of workers in mining, manufacturing, construction, and domestic service were black. Whites were the majority only in commerce and transport and communication. Colored and African women made up 76 percent of the domestic workers.

A. Anti-Apartheid Events

1940s	Organizing African, Colored, and multi-racial unions.
1940s	Communist Party members elected to municipal and provincial councils and to Parliament (Natives' Representatives).
1940–1948	Opposition by Natives' Representative Council to the Pass Laws.
1941	National Anti-Pass Conference.
1942	Council of Non-European Trade Unions formed.
1942	African strikes.
1943	Marabastad Riot (16 Africans shot).
1943	Conference for a People's Charter, Resolution demanding recognition of Africans as employees and national minimum wage of R4 ($5.60) per week.

1943	ANC Anti-Pass Campaign.
1943	Joint Committee of European and African Women formed.
1943	All-African Convention to establish the Non-European Unity Movement (in competition with the NEUF).
1944	Campaign for Right and Justice (churches, trade unions, ANC).
1945	All-In Conference of the Non-White Trade Unions.
1946	Springbok Legion founded to oppose the Grey Shirts.
1946	African MineWorkers Union strike.
1946	Indian Passive Resistance Campaign in Durban.
1947	African Trade Unions Technical Advisory Committee formed.
1948	Formation of the ANC activist Youth League.
1948	ANC Programme of Action to achieve National Freedom.
1949	Cape District of the CP call for a general strike to oppose apartheid.

B. The Role of Women in Anti-Apartheid Organizations Trade Unions

The trade union organizing by women of women and black industrial workers begun in the twenties and thirties reached its peak during the forties. The tobacco workers', laundry and dry cleaning workers', waitresses', garment workers', and food and canning workers' unions all continued or obtained Industrial Conciliation Council agreements. The African Mine Workers Union was the only other major union (other than those for white craftsmen) being organized, but could not be formally recognized. The unions with Afrikaner women as members and leaders continued to resist the Afrikaner Nationalist efforts - many times violent - to take over their unions. These unions remained affiliated with the SAT&LC and their leaders served as members of the national executive of the SAT&LC.

Political Parties. In the forties women continued to play a small role in the leadership of the Communist Party in South Africa. Several women ran for office, as Communist Party candidates, winning seats on the Cape Town Municipal Council and on the Johannesburg City Council. When the Government arrested the national CP Central Executive Committee in 1946, this included two women, both of whom were then also elected municipal officials. Members of the CP continued to be objects of Government legal action to restrict their activities, and meetings organized by the CP were consistently prohibited.

The Labor Party elected a woman as their Chair and ran the same woman successfully for Mayor of Johannesburg in 1945.

Non-White National Organizations. In the late forties both women and youth came into their own in the ANC, but only by forming their own organizations. Women still were not an integral part of the ANC, but they were the organizers of the ANC demonstrations and anti-pass campaigns.

The Non-European Unity Movement (NEUM) was formed at the Unity Conference in Bloemfontein in December 1943, through efforts of the Communist Party. The purpose was to unite non-European opposition to white domination. The ANC and the South African Indian Congress did not participate. However, the ANC had been a member of NEUM's forerunner, the All-African Convention, formed in December 1935 in Bloemfontein to oppose the Hertzog Bills. The NEUM called for

1. Universal suffrage of all men and women over 21.
2. Compulsory free and uniform education to age 16, with free meals, books, etc. for the needy.
3. Inviolability of persons, homes, and privacy.
4. Freedom of speech, press, and association.
5. Freedom of movement and of occupation.
6. Equality of rights, with no distinction because of race, sex, or color.
7. Boycott of the Natives' Representative Council and of separate parliamentary seats elections. (Joshi, pp. 99-100)

The all-male Natives' Representative Council had found itself totally ineffective and, therefore, decided to end the charade in 1946.

The Indian Passive Resistance Campaign, organized by the South African Indian Congress (SAIC), included a number of women leaders and participants. The women spent many days in jail, and helped each other out by looking after children and homes while the parents "resisted." The South African Indian Organization was formed in 1947 to counter the "radicalism" of the SAIC, and had no place for women.

Interracial Organizations. The SAIRR expanded its research and education activities in the forties, preparing reports and studies, and operating education programs. Through these efforts the SAIRR opposed interference by the Government with the autonomy of trade unions and the separation of workers by race. In the forties the first women were chosen as life members of the SAIRR, the position of Honorary Organizer for the Women's Section was abolished, and several women were elected to the Executive Committee.

The Campaign for Right and Justice, organized in 1944 and involving women and men in its leadership, sought

1. Drastic measures against profiteering, particularly in the production and distribution of food and clothing.
2. Full-scale development of the industrial and human resources of the country.
3. Provision of social services for all races, particularly in the areas of health care, housing, education, and unemployment insurance.
4. Fulfillment of obligations to members of the armed forces and their dependents.

The campaign leaders called for full and direct representation of all sections of the community; for the abolition of all legislation discriminatory on grounds of color, race, or sex; for provision of land for the landless and assistance in making the best use of it; and for a minimum working wage of ₤2 per week. (A Time

to Speak, M. Scott, pp. 114-115)
The Anglican Church, mainly through Michael Scott, Arthur Blaxall, and Bishop S.W. Lavis, took its place in the forties in the anti-apartheid movement. Scott participated in the Indian Passive Resistance Campaign and chaired the Campaign for Right and Justice for one year. He also participated in the Conference for a People's Charter. Blaxall and Scott helped raise funds for African trade unions. Since the churches had no place for women except in auxiliaries and service groups, women played no role in church leadership decisions affecting participation in the anti-apartheid movement. However, the above named men did work closely with women involved in the movement.

The Christian Council, a multi-racial group of affiliated churches, sent a deputation to testify before a Government commission urging the abolition of passes and treatment of Africans as responsible members of society. Again, women had no leadership role.

C. Individual Women in the Anti-Apartheid Movement

During the forties most of the women leaders in the anti-apartheid movement were trade union organizers and leaders. During the decade these women organized several multi-racial unions, usually serving as general secretary of at least one:

Dulcie Marie Hartwell - garment workers, building workers
Johanna Cornelius - garment workers, tobacco workers
Anna Elizabeth Scheepers - garment workers, sweet and
    tobacco workers
Katie Viljoen - garment workers
Joey Fourie - waitresses
Ray Alexander - food and canning workers
Bettie du Toit - textile, canning, chemical, laundry and
    dry cleaning workers
Nancy Dick - textile workers

Other women trade union organizers included Katie la Grange, Pauline Podbrey, and Koetie Augustyn on the Cape, organizing mainly non-European factory and shop workers; Hester Cornelius, Sannie van Wyk, Johanna Breitenbach, Rose de Freitas, and Margaret Malan on the Witwatersrand; Nora Forsyth, catering workers; and Katie Kagan, distributive workers. Beila Page succeeded Ms. Kagan as secretary of the National Union of Distributive Workers.

All these unions had a large female membership except the Laundry and Dry Cleaning Workers, who were mainly African and Indian men, and the Chemical (edible oil and soap) Workers, mainly African men. And these "mixed" unions maintained formal participation in the SAT&LC in the hope of changing the all white male craft unions and so developing a unified trade union movement in South Africa. Bettie du Toit, Johanna Cornelius, Anna Scheepers, Dulcie Hartwell, and Beila Page all served on the National Executive Committee of the SAT&LC in the forties. Katie Viljoen, secretary of the Port Elizabeth branch of the Garment Workers Union, served as secretary of the Eastern Province Local Committee of the SAT&LC.

These industrial unions organized by the women had two major problems in the forties: (1) the Afrikaner Nationalists identified trade unions with communism and wanted to make the unions with Afrikaner members part of the National Socialism of the F.A.K., and (2) so many blacks sought jobs in the urban areas that educating them not to serve as scab labor was virtually impossible.

When Bettie du Toit went early in the 1940s to Paarl, an Afrikaner community in the Cape, to organize Afrikaner women textile workers, she came into direct contact with Afrikaaner Nationalism, through the Dutch Reformed Church (DRC). Ms. du Toit first obtained a job as a weaver in the factory, and a room in the hostel run for the workers by the DRC. Gradually she began to organize the women. To maintain her sanity she frequently would spend the weekend with friends in Cape Town.

Soon the DRC discovered she was organizing a trade union. They began preaching in the churches against her, saying that a terrible communist was in their midst organizing; that she believed in free love and opposed personal property; and that she would destroy the morality of the fine Afrikaner girls. The predicants urged that she be driven out of Paarl.

Her room was searched and books on nationalism and colonialism found. The next day at work the workers threw their trade union cards at her and acted in a threatening manner. The factory manager called her in and asked if she had been organizing a trade union. When she replied that she had, he asked if she knew the girls planned to beat her up after work. She had known, and she was terrified. But she returned to her place and continued weaving, her knees trembling. They left her alone, and she was not touched when she left.

She was totally ostracized by the community. When whe got on a bus, everyone got off. When she walked down the street, everyone crossed to the other side. She could find no other living quarters. Still she decided to continue working and to try to convince the women she was not an enemy. The Africans, too, moved away from her as readily as the whites. They were afraid to show sympathy since she had not shown any willingness to organize them, having determined from previous experience to organize the whites first and then to work on their racial prejudices.

Without a place to live Ms. du Toit was forced to return to Cape Town. Soon after her departure the DRC and the Nationalist Party organized a mass meeting in the Paarl City Hall. Bettie du Toit learned of the mass meeting when the Secretary for Labor, Ivan Walker, asked her to come talk with him. He, a member of Smuts' Government, told her she "had to go to the meeting." Apparently the "greyshirts" wanted to use the meeting to destroy any chance of a trade union surviving at the factory. Joey Fourie, the organizer of the waitresses, agreed to accompany her.

During the meeting the Afrikaner farmers began asking who and where was this terrible woman. Ms. du Toit stood up and spoke. The farmers asked how such a pretty woman could be evil. The farmers did not give the Nationalists any support, and the meeting ended keeping the "status quo" - no union and no beatings by the "greyshirts." (from personal interview)

The Garment Workers Union in Port Elizabeth, headed by Katie Viljoen, had about 800 members in 1939, half of whom were Colored. The Nationalists managed to convert a few of the white members and had them agitate within the union against the leaders, especially E.S. Sachs (a Jew and General Secretary). These women would harrass Sachs by doing such things as greeting him by shouting "Heil Hitler." (Rebels Daughters, Sachs, p. 140) The ministers of the DRC would preach against the unions and then would visit the factories and incite tensions between the European and non-European workers.

On March 16, 1944, the GWU called a mass meeting in Johannesburg, attended by some 5000 union members. Nationalists tried to break up the meeting by force, using bicycle chains, sticks, and one, a knife. The women stewards succeeded in throwing them out, not without injury to several of the union members, and the GWU went on with its meeting. The Union maintained a legal counter-attack throughout this period and consistently won in the courts.

But hostility toward the multi-racail and non-white unions was not unique to the Nationalists. The African Mine Workers Union found no responsiveness in the Smuts Government to their attempts to improve the wages and working conditions of mineworkers, which eventually ended in the massive strike in 1946, arrest of the union leaders, and arrest of the entire Executive Committee of the Communist Party, which was accused of being responsible for the strike.

The Durban laundry and dry cleaning workers had their efforts to increase wages in 1944 broken by use of African scab workers. Only when the Johannesburg Laundry and Dry Cleaning Workers' Union, of which Ms. du Toit was Secretary, obtained an Industrial Conciliation Council agreement which could be extended to the Durban workers did their situation improve. Bettie du Toit had been called to Durban in 1944 by the union to help organize and run the strike, which ended in her arrest, being charged with incitement to public violence, and imprisonment. The strike caused serious deprivation for the workers, relieved at Christmas time by Canadian sailors sharing their food supplies.

Ms. du Toit also assisted the Indian union organizers and the Indian Congress in Natal in collecting information on the conditions of the sugar cane workers. A presentation was made to the South African Trades and Labor Council Executive Council to urge that action be taken: men, women, and children were working up to 14 hours a day and living in hovels with no furniture or sanitary facilities. (Ms. du Toit also worked without success to have African workers included under the Unemployment Insurance Act.)

In 1940 Johanna Cornelius had been asked to help organize the predominantly male Afrikaner tobacco workers in Rustenburg in the Transvaal. At that time they earned a maximum of R2.25 ($3.15) per week. The Afrikaners were under pressure from the Nationalists to divide along racial lines. The workers eventually went on strike. Both Cornelius and du Toit were arrested during the strike and imprisoned.

The Food and Canning Workers' Union in the Cape, under the leadership of Ray Alexander, obtained a 45-hour work week, two weeks paid holiday, and ten-minute breaks in the morning and in the afternoon. When in 1947 the Union was forced to exclude African members, an African union was formed, and Ms. Alexander served as General Secretary of both unions. In 1951 she was banned from all trade union activity.

With the increased activity of the Afrikaner Nationalists in the forties and the increase in apartheid legislation, national non-white and multi-racial organizations initiated more actions opposing the legislation and calling for a complete change in direction. Many of the women trade union leaders participated in these organizations and activities and ran as political candidates, but the multi-racial and African and Colored unions themselves refrained from taking political stands.

Within the ANC movement had begun to "stop talking and start acting." Key to this effort were the young people who formed the Youth League, including Vivien Ncakeni and Albertina Sisulu (then not married) along with several future leaders of the ANC - Oliver Tambo, Walter Sisulu, and Nelson Mandela. The thrust of the League was to made the ANC a national movement. Much as Charlotte Maxeke (who died in 1939) had urged in the 1920s that Africans become independent of white sympathisers, though cooperating with them, so the leaders of the Youth League called for African leadership and action, but not separatist black racialism. Vivien Ncakeni was the only woman among the six leading proponents of this position.

In 1943 Madie-Hall Xuma, an American married to Dr. A.B. Xuma, then President of the ANC, was elected President of the ANC Women's Section. Ms. Xuma was particularly active in moves to attain cooperation among various organizations, improved education, and economic self-sufficiency. She was followed in 1948 by Ida Mtwana. Neither was involved in organizing African women, so the Women's Section remained dormant.

Cissie Gool continued in the early forties as president of the Non-European Unity Front and the National Liberation League, and served on the Cape Town City Council from her initial election in 1938 until 1954. The unity in opposition to apartheid she had sought to achieve never came to fruition, and she was never recognized as a national leader.

With the proposal in 1946 to restrict Indians to certain geographical areas and to remove them from the common voter rolls, Indians began their own Passive Resistance campaign in Durban. Each night six resisters would try to camp on a plot of land set aside for white occupation. The white English-speaking community in Durban expressed extreme hostility, and white gangs attacked the resisters while the police turned their backs. Several women led groups of resisters, some consisting completely of women. Mononmoney Naidoo spent 30 days in jail during the Campaign; Ellapen Naicker was imprisoned twice; Amina Pahad, Miriam Cachalia, and Dr. Zainap Asvat also led resistors, were imprisoned, and helped raise funds for the families of other resisters while they were in prison.

The Indians requested support from other organizations, and Bettie du Toit - representing the trade unions, Michael Scott - the churches, and Benny Sission - students, went to Durban. The Durban whites became more incensed at the white supporters of the Indians, especially Ms. du Toit, than at the Indians. In one incident it was only because a police wagon drove up and she managed to get in that Ms. du Toit escaped serious injury.

As candidates and political activists women played a more direct role in the anti-apartheid movement than they could play within organizations, except in the trade unions.

Johanna Cornelius and Anna Scheepers of the GWU both ran for Parliament unsuccessfully, as Independent Labor Party candidates on a platform of "progressive capitalism." Katie Viljoen of the GWU served two terms on the Port Elizabeth City Council. Joey Fourie, the Afrikaans woman who had organized the waitresses in the Cape in the late thirties, and then later served as General Secretary of the Cape Town branch of the National Union of Distributive Workers, won a seat in 1945 on the Cape Town City Council as a Communist Party candidate. Ronnie Fleet, Secretary of the Hairdressers Union and of the Rand Committee of the Trades and Labor Council, also ran as a Communist Party candidate.

Johanna Cornelius and Dulcie Hartwell served on the Executive Council of the Labor Party. Jessie McPherson, a trade unionist, was elected Mayor of Johannesburg in 1946, the only woman Mayor of Johannesburg, and served for many years as Chair of the South African Labor Party. As Mayor Ms. McPherson urged the Government to negotiate with the African Mine Workers Union, to recognize African unions, and to deal with the real economic grievances of the African miners. In 1946 Jessie McPherson became a founding member of the Springbok Legion, formed to prevent the election of a fascist government in South Africa and to obtain increased pay for those who served in the armed forces during World War II. In 1945 she was made the only patron of the Legion.

In 1945 Hilda Watts was the only Communist elected to the Johannesburg City Council, for which she chaired the Native Affairs Department. During an argument in the Council over expulsion of "squatters" from Orlando township, Ms. Watts accused Labor Party Council members of racism and support of undemocratic deportations and was one of two Council members to oppose the expulsion. Ms. Watts also served on the Executive Committee of the Anti-Fascist Movement, and was one of the members of the National Executive Committee of the Communist Party who were arrested in 1946 and 1947 and charged with sedition following the African Mine Workers Union strike.

The other female member of the Executive Committee of the Communist Party who was arrested in 1946 was Betty Radford Sacks. Ms. Sacks had joined the Communist Party in 1941, after having started the Guardian, later the official organ of the Communist Party, in 1937. She edited the Guardian without pay for eleven years, raising the circulation to 50,000. Ms. Sacks served on the Cape Town City Council from 1943-1946, and was a member of the Central Executive Committee of the CPSA from 1946-1948.

Ray Alexander, General Secretary of the Food and Canning

Workers' Union, was also a member of the CPSA Central Executive Committee in the forties. Joan Rose-Innes Findlay served as secretary of the Pretoria District of the Communist Party; and Molly Krige Fischer, related to the Smuts family and wife of Bram Fischer, ran for the Johannesburg City Council as the Communist Party candidate for Hillbrow-Berea, a section of Johannesburg.

Margaret Ballinger retained her seat in Parliament as the Cape Eastern Natives' Representative throughout the decade. She supported the African Mine Workers Union and urged the Government to negotiate. Then in 1949 the Government prohibited her from holding meetings in the townships around Johannesburg.

During the forties another member of the Communist Party Executive, Ruth First, along with the Revd. Michael Scott, conducted the farm labor investigations at Bethal which ended in the expose of Government use of prison labor and victims of apartheid legislation as cheap or free labor for farmers. Ms. First worked as a reporter for the Guardian, and edited Fighting Talk, another CP publication. She had joined the Communist Party as a student, and remained a leader of the Party.

Dr. Ellen Hellmann of the South African Institute of Race Relations was the only woman among the twelve people who formed the African Trade Unions Technical Advisory Committee to assist African trade unions in collection of funds, obtaining necessary information, and taking legal actions. Dr. Hellmann also conducted research and prepared several publications on the wages and conditions of black workers in South Africa. Dr. Hellmann edited the Handbook on Race Relations in South Africa published by the Oxford University Press in Cape Town in 1949 (778 pages).

Several other women were active in the SAIRR in the 1940s: Eleanor Hawarden prepared the pamphlet, "Labor and the NEP," published by the Institute in 1942; Maida Whyte directed the Institute's literacy program, which in the forties received financial support from the Government, to provide adult education to reduce the educational disparity among the races; in 1949 Edith Rheinallt Jones announced her ten-year plan to achieve free and compulsory primary education for Africans; Clare Rheinallt Jones organized study circles for the Institute as a means of public education; Helen Suzman conducted research; Winnifred Hoernle' testified before the Fagan Commission - set up to investigate the conditions of non-whites - that the African people were weary of suffering, of crowded housing, of restrictions imposed by discriminatory laws, of removals, and under such conditions violence could be expected.

Dr. Elsi Chubb, Mrs. W.A.D. Russell, Margaret Ballinger, Dr. Ellen Hellmann, and Dr. Sheila van der Horst served on the Executive Committee of the SAIRR during the decade, and Mrs. W.F. Grant chaired the Cape Western Regional Committee. Dr. Nellie Spilhaus, Edith Rheinallt Jones, and Winnifred Hoernle' were elected to life membership in the SAIRR, the first women so honored.

The various individual South African women who played vital roles in the anti-apartheid movement in the forties, especially in the multi-racial unions, in the SAIRR, in the CPSA and related organizations, and as elected officials, had little impact on the

overall power structure in South Africa. As in the twenties and
thirties the anti-apartheid "movement" was not a movement but a
number of individuals and organizations opposing various pieces
of the discriminatory legislation and practices adopted by the
South African Government. No one was able to put together a united
front: unions were split among themselves, with the white craft
unions supporting the color bar; the African, Colored, and Indian
national organizations were going through internal turmoil over
whether or not to directly oppose the Government; and the political
parties, except the Communist Party, continually backed down before
the pressures for apartheid legislation. The women's activities
appear to have had little impact on the traditional anti-apartheid
organizations, but the women were crucial to the continuation and
expansion of opposition to apartheid. The women, by being totally
removed from the power structure - economic, political (with the
above exceptions), religious, and social - had no false image of
better times to come. They saw, they reported, and they protested
things which the men refused to recognize. Still the Nationalists
obtained control of the Government in 1948 with a minority vote,
and the lines of battle over apartheid and discrimination, over
civil rights and civil liberties, became more clearly drawn.

CHAPTER 6

VI. THE FIFTIES

The full intent of the apartheid ideology was realized with
passage and enforcement of the Suppression of Communism Act (SCA)
(1950), the Group Areas Act requiring residential segregation
(1950), and the Abolition of Pass Laws and Coordination of Documents Act (1952). Through these Acts the Government gained the
authority (1) to ban anyone seeking to change the economic or
political structure of South Africa, i.e. anyone opposed to
apartheid; (2) to endorse out of an urban area any African who
caused any trouble, i.e. organized demonstrations, trade unions,
political groups; (3) to maintain a monthly accounting of every
African male by requiring his reference book be signed by his
employer every month and be on his person at all times; and (4)
to extend the pass laws to women (for the first time since the
1920s). By adding these powers to those provided through "influx
control" legislation, the Government obtained complete authority
over the residence, employment, assembly, and movement of Africans
living outside the Reserves.

The Communist Party of South Africa dissolved itself prior
to passage of the SCA, and re-formed underground in 1953 as the
South African Communist Party. (From this point on it is almost
impossible to determine membership in the Party.)

In 1954 instead of amending the Industrial Conciliation Act
to include African men in the definition of employee as had been
requested by all the anti-apartheid organizations, the Government
decided to exclude African women. Immediately upon passage of the
Act some employers reduced African women's wages and began to
replace European women with Africans. The multi-racial unions
were able to stop this through enforcement of Industrial Council
agreements, but coordinated action by workers of all races became
even more difficult.

The list of restrictive legislation passed in the fifties is
long. Much of it only tightened provisions of existing legislation, but two of the new Acts, the Separate Representation of
Voters Act (1951) and the Bantu Education Act (1953), had a
particularly destructive impact on blacks. The first Act removed
the Colored voters from the common rolls and gave the Coloreds
four white representatives in Parliament beginning in 1958. The
second Act gave the Government complete control over all schools
with African students, including the power to decide who will
teach children and what they will teach. The Government's
curriculum, developed by the Afrikaner Nationalists, was called
Christian National Education, and had as its object to inculcate
in the children belief in the absolute superiority of the white
race and of the Afrikaner culture.

Additional legislation which had a major impact on South
African society was the South Africa Act Amendment Act of 1956,

which stated that no court of law can inquire into or pronounce upon the validity of any law passed by Parliament. The Act was used to remove the Coloreds from the common voting roll, a major victory of the executive over the judicial branch, a battle which had continued since the 18th century. The Promotion of Bantu Self-Government Act of 1959 abolished the representation of Cape African men, who, since 1936 had elected three white members of Parliament, and instead recognized eight African national units.

The legislation and the resulting intensification of apartheid and abrogation of civil rights and civil liberties brought a massive response from anti-apartheid organizations, who again tried to unite into one movement, the Congress movement. The Government had succeeded in making every organization and every individual who opposed the Government's position on race and on Afrikaner superiority subject to complete deprivation of rights and livelihood.

The first united effort was the Defiance Campaign of 1952, organized by the ANC and the SAIC, which involved passive defiance of apartheid laws and resulted in the arrest and imprisonment of approximately 8,000 Africans. Very few whites and Indians participated.

In 1955 the Congress of the People was held, following which the participating organizations began a campaign to obtain two million signatures to the Freedom Charter presented at the Congress. The Government responded in December when the police arrested 156 of the Congress leaders and charged them with treason. The resultant Treason Trials, beginning in 1956, finally ended in 1961 with charges being dropped or findings of not guilty.

In 1959 a group within the ANC opposed to the Congress movement and to working with former communists broke away and formed the Pan-African Congress (PAC), under the leadership of Robert Sobukwe.

In 1955 about 3,000 white women formed the Women's Defense of the Constitution League, known as the Black Sash. The purpose of the organization upon formation was to oppose the stacking of the Senate by the Nationalists through use of unconstitutional means in order to obtain removal of Colored men from the common voting roll. The Black Sash collected the signatures of 100,000 white women on a petition asking the Governor General not to sign the bill.

The trade union movement went through several reorganizations in the fifties. In 1950 several white unions disaffiliated from the SAT&LC and formed the pro-apartheid South African Federation of Trade Unions. The Federation had 23 affiliates by 1954 with 100,000 members. In 1957 the Federation joined with the Federal Consultative Council of the South African Railways and the Coordinating Council of South African Trade Unions (formed in 1959) to form the South African Confederation of Labor. Following prohibition of multi-racial unions by the Government in 1953, the SAT&LC dissolved in 1954 and re-formed as the Trade Union Council of South Africa (TUCSA), including for the first time a color bar in the constitution. As a result the unions which wanted to remain integrated and the Non-European Trade Union Federation (NTUF) formed the South African Congress of Trade Unions, and the African unions which opposed any association with the communists formed the Federation of Free Trade Unions of South Africa (FOFATUSA). (TUCSA had included in the 1954 constitution statement of purpose dedication to "opposing communism in all its forms.")

By 1958 TUCSA had 46 affiliated unions plus six African unions in liaison, totaling 192,590 members; SACTU had 27 affiliates with 20,187 members; the South African Confederation of Labor, 32 affiliates with 144,354 members; and FOFATUSA, 17 affiliates with 18,000 members. Another 48 unions with 75,907 members had no affiliation. A total of only 451,038 workers belonged to unions, yet in 1960 over 1.1 million whites alone were "economically active."

In 1951 the National and the Afrikaner parties amalgamated, and in 1953 won 94 seats in Parliament, an increase of 15 seats and 155,000 votes over the 1948 election. The United Party lost 8 seats but received 50,000 more votes than in 1948, and only 22,000 less votes than the National Party. In 1954 Dr. Malan retired at the age of 84, and J.G. Strijdom became Prime Minister. Strijdom died in 1958, four months after the election, and Dr. H.F. Verwoerd became the Prime Minister. In the 1958 election the National Party increased its majority by winning 103 seats (642,000 votes) against the United Party's 53 seats (504,000 votes).

The United Party adopted policies in the fifties which allowed them to vote for nearly every piece of apartheid legislation. In reaction to this whites finding no choice between the major parties formed first the Liberal Party and then the Federal Party in 1953 and the Progressive Party in 1959.

The Liberal Party platform called for maintenance of the rule of law, the essential dignity of every human being, opposition of totalitarianism - Communism and Fascism, and extension of the franchise to all qualified South African citizens (those who had completed Standard Six and had an income of R500 or more per year). The Liberal Party welcomed members of all races. (The Liberal Party dissolved itself in 1968 just prior to passage of legislation forbidding multi-racial political parties.)

The Federal Party announced its goals to be

> to create in South Africa opportunities for people
> of all races to enjoy fulness of life and liberty
> under the protection of the law...; to provide a
> Constitution...as a basis for the future Federal
> Union of the States and Territories of Southern
> Africa;...to reshape within the Act of Union the
> present quasi-unitary system to one of Federal
> Union;...to maintain the present system of limited
> group representation of Natives"

but to move toward the ultimate goal of placing qualified non-Europeans on the common voter roll. The Party endorsed economic integration and social segregation. (Race Relations Memorandum 104/53; 15.7.53)

The Progressive Party opposed the pass law and influx systems, but proposed controls on movement of workers between urban and rural areas. They also opposed the reference book requirements for Africans, proposing a simple identification system similar to drivers' licenses, for all citizens.

During the fifties while the Government was pressing for segregation, yet allowing use of cheap African labor by white employers, the number of Africans in the urban areas continued to increase. By 1951 the number of whites in urban areas had increased to 2.0 million; of Africans, to 2.3 million. And by 1960, 2.46 million whites lived in urban areas, and 3.2 million Africans. So the gap between actual numbers of whites and Africans in urban areas increased from 115,000 more whites than Africans in 1936 to 700,000 more Africans than whites in 1960. In addition 1.32 million Coloreds and Asians were living in urban areas in 1960.

In 1955 the Government Commission on the Socio-Economic Development of Native Areas within the Union of South Africa stated a choice must be made either to have complete integration or to enforce separate development. The Commission recommended the latter and proposed a plan for development of the Reserves/ Bantustans/Homelands. The Government chose the method of "border industries" as the first step toward bringing urban industry to the Reserves' labor force. Not until the 1960s did this policy begin to result in a material change in the location of jobs. Meanwhile, the Government required massive removals of Africans and Asians from urban areas, from African townships which had become too close to expanding white neighborhoods, and from areas declared white.

Parallel to the changes in urban versus rural population, the percent of the national income obtained from manufacturing increased from 17.6 percent in 1938 to 24.5 percent in 1958; from mining, decreased from 19.5 percent in 1938 to 12.9 percent in 1958; from finance, increased from 2.1 to 3.6 percent and from transportation, increased from 6.7 to 8.1 percent. (van den Berghe, p. 300)

The gap between white and non-white wages increased in the fifties. Whereas in 1946-47 the ratio reached a low of 1:3.54, by 1958-59 the ratio had increased to 1:4.8. (van den Berghe, p. 305) Africans experienced a 6.5 percent decrease in their standard of living between 1938-39 and 1953-54, while Asians and Coloreds had an 11 percent increase, and whites a 46 percent increase. (van den Berghe, p. 304)

A. Anti-Apartheid Events

1950	Protests against the Suppression of Communism Act.
1950	Communist Party of South Africa dissolved. Re-formed underground in 1953 as the South African Communist Party.
26.6.50	ANC National Day of Protest and Mourning.
1951	Establishment of the Franchise Action Council, Cape Town.
1951	Formation of the Torch Commando, which evolved into the United Federal Party in 1953, to encourage federation with neighboring territories.
1952	Defiance Against Unjust Laws campaign (ANC).
5.52	Guardian banned, replaced successively by New Age and The Clarion.

43

1953	South African Liberal Party formed.
1953	South African Colored People's Organization (SACPO) formed.
1953-55	Anti-Bantu Education campaign. Formation of cultural organizations.
1954	Formation of the Federation of Free African Trade Unions of South Africa (FOFATUSA), allied with the SAT&LC.
1954	Formation of the Federation of South African Women, affiliated with the Women's International Democratic Federation.
1955	Formation of the South African Congress of Trade Unions (SACTU), absorbing the Non-European Trade Union Federation (NTUF).
June 25-26 1955	Congress of the People, Kliptown. Adoption of the Freedom Charter. (June 26 became South African Freedom Day.)
1955	Formation of the Women's Defense of the Constitution League (the Black Sash).
1955	Transvaal anti-pass demonstration by the Women's Federation in the Transvaal (mainly African women).
1956	Johannesburg/Alexandra Bus Boycott resulting from a fare increase.
1956	Protest in Pretoria by 20,000 women against the pass laws. Presented grievances and demands to the Prime Minister. Beginning of South Africa's Women's Day.
1956-61	Treason Trials with 156 defendants.
1957	Women's demonstration against the Bantu Authorities Act and extension of passes to women in Zeerust/Sekhukhuniland and Dinokane. ANC banned in the Province.
1958	Women's demonstrations in Johannesburg against the Sophiatown removal. Mass arrests.
1959	Protests by women in Umzinto and Ixopo, Natal, including destruction of 75 percent of the dipping tanks.
1959	ANC Potato Boycott because of use of convict labor and low wages.
1959	Women refused to accept passes when issued to them in Natal, the Cape, and the Transvaal.
1959	Pan-African Congress founded (anti-communist), breakaway group from ANC.
1959	Progressive Party formed.

B. The Role of Women in Anti-Apartheid Organizations Trade Unions

The anti-apartheid trade unions suffered even more disruption in the fifties than in the forties. Women continued to play a major role in trade union leadership and organizing, and the unions involving the majority of women members were affiliated either with the TUCSA or SACTU. When the Government prohibited mixed trade unions in 1959, several of these unions with a high percentage of women members either applied for special permission to keep mixed membership or set up separate branches by race. Both TUCSA and SACTU had women officers and for much of the 1950s the general secretary of each was a woman.

A number of women trade union leaders were banned under the Suppression of Communism Act in the fifties and prohibited from participating in union activities. The majority of these women were associated with SACTU, whose main goals were to

1. obtain legal recognition of all trade unions;
2. abolish the industrial color bar and racial discrimination in all spheres of social, economic, cultural, and political life;
3. abolish the pass system;
4. gain the right for all workers to choose the best job on the best market; and
5. secure a national minimum wage of R2 ($2.80) per day.

Twenty-three of the 156 defendants in the Treason Trials were SACTU officials.

African women workers conducted several illegal strikes in the 1950s, usually ending with their being arrested. For example, in Johannesburg in 1959, 288 canning workers went on strike for having to work Christmas Day. The police and the Government opposed the employers' efforts to negotiate with the African workers or unions.

Non-white National Organizations. The leadership and the official membership of every non-white national organization - the African National Congress, the South African Indian Congress, the South African Colored People's Organization, the Pan African Congress - were predominantly, if not completely, male. The ANC, though still maintaining the separate Women's League, did for the first time make the League president a member of the National Executive Committee. Every one of these organizations, however, except the PAC, depended upon women to organize and participate in their various campaigns, demonstrations, and boycotts. In the fifties the women organized themselves more extensively than at any time since the anti-pass campaigns in the 1920s, and ran their own programs, with or without the support or participation of the men. Women were integral to the 1952 Defiance Campaign, the Bantu Education boycott from 1953-1955, the 1955 Congress of the People, the 1956 Alexandra Bus Boycott, the Zeerust anti-pass demonstrations in 1957, the protests surrounding the 1958 Sophiatown removals, and the movement in Natal against removals, passes, rent increases, lack of employment permits, poll tax, and the regulations requiring women to fill the dipping tanks without pay. Several of these campaigns resulted in hundreds of women being confined in jail.

The 1954 passage of the Bantu Education Act brought resistance from African women to having their children's education dominated by the Christian Nationalist white supremacist philosophy. Women in the ANC led the school boycott, to which the Government responded by refusing to allow these children to attend school. Under Bantu Education the African children could be taught only in their "trigal" language, and, therefore, had to attend a "tribal" school. The Africans made every attempt to teach the children English, and to maintain some integrity in the education system. Anger at the Bantu

Education system was so high that in 1959 several schools were
burned during riots. The National Education Movement, which incorporated the cultural clubs set up in opposition to Bantu Education,
was founded and run by African women. The ANC endorsed the opposition to Bantu Education, but viewed the education of children as
the concern of women. The Movement was disbanded by police action.

The Alexandra bus boycott was also organized mainly by the
women of the ANC. The boycott, resulting from a penny increase in
bus fare, required workers to walk 9 miles to Johannesburg for 3
months before the increase was dropped.

Political Parties. The newly formed Liberal and Progressive
Parties included women as well as men as members, and both elected
a woman as their first president. The Communist Party did not
play a public role as a political party in the fifties, though
many women were banned under the Suppression of Communism Act.

Multi-racial Organizations. In the fifties the South African
Institute of Race Relations involved more women in its leadership
and regional organizations than in earlier decades. The Institute
did not participate in the anti-apartheid events, but it did report
on them. As stated in its initial purpose, the Institute continued
"to promote interracial cooperation and the use of democratic
procedures, to develop common loyalties to our country, and to
discourage the emergence of any exclusive sectional or racial
nationalism." (RR 79/57; 23.4.57) Their method continued to be
research, publication, and multi-racial conferences and seminars.
Then in 1957 the 46 members of the Institute's National Executive
Committee, eight of whom were women, issued a release stating

> No people can be kept in the strait-jacket of control
> which the legislation of the past nine years added to
> an already repressive legislative structure, has
> imposed, and which the Bills at present before Parlia-
> ment - the Native Laws Amendment Bill and the Separate
> University Education Bill - make even more intolerable.
>
> These Bills, taken together with the directives being
> issued to welfare organizations, aim at undermining
> all voluntary European association with Africans and
> canalising all contact through public servants alone.
> Should this happen and should the tide of resentment,
> now running, continue, then we believe most sincerely
> that the outcome will be tragic for all in our country.
> With means of voluntary communication increasingly
> restricted, the racial groups may become sealed off
> into entirely separate and hostile camps.

During the fifties a fourth woman was elected to life membership, and the Institute elected for the first time a woman as
the head, and two women vice-chairmen.

The churches became more involved in anti-apartheid efforts
in the fifties through their showdown with the Government over
"Clause 29" of the proposed Native Laws Amendment Act which would
have enforced apartheid on the churches. The Church of the Province

of South Africa (Anglican) led the response by writing the Prime Minister to tell him the Anglican clergy would be ordered to disobey if the Act were passed. As a result the Clause was withdrawn. But in the churches' efforts to oppose apartheid women played a minimal role. The Mothers Union of the Anglican Church made more efforts to hold multi-racial meetings and to develop social welfare programs, but they had no place in the hierarchy. The same pattern occurred in the Methodist and Roman Catholic churches, the clergy of which were even less involved in opposition to apartheid.

Both the SAIRR and clergy from the Anglican Church participated in publicizing the removals of Africans and in setting up the Treason Trial Defense Fund.

As women in the various non-white national organizations began to organize themselves into their own politically active groups, so women from these and white organizations determined to come together to form the Federation of South African Women. The conference to found the Federation included about 150 delegates from various organizations claiming to represent 230,000 women. The Women's Charter drawn up at the conference set the goal of the Federation to abolish "all laws, regulations, conventions and customs that discriminate against women" and "to unite women in common action for the removal of all disabilities." (RR Survey, 1953-54, p. 13) The Federation participated in the Congress of the People and organized several massive anti-pass demonstrations, the largest one in October 1956 involving 20,000 women. During this demonstration the women presented petitions to the Prime Minister (only his Secretary appeared to receive the petitions) demanding better housing, general free education, free hospitalization, elimination of the pass, and general adult suffrage. By May of 1956 several thousand women who had received passes had held demonstrations at which they burned their pass books. These demonstrations had included 1200 women in Germiston, 2000 in Sophiatown and Newclare, 4000 in Pretoria, and several hundred in other areas.

Several whites, women and men - many of whom had formerly been members of the Communist Party - opposed to apartheid formed the Congress of Democrats (COD). The COD members separated themselves from the whites in the Liberal and Progressive parties by endorsing the ANC position of full and universal suffrage. The stated purpose of the COD was to establish "...a new South Africa based on a democratic system where men and women of all races will enjoy equal opportunities in all fields of life." ("Face of the Future," COD, 1960)

Together the ANC, SAIC, SACPO, SACTU, and COD formed the "Congress Movement" to oppose white supremacy and apartheid. The Congress Movement organized the Congress of the People (COP) held on June 25 and 26, 1955, at Kliptown, with 2000 Africans, 300 Indians, 300 Coloreds, and 200 whites participating. Members of the Congress organizations had contacted blacks throughout South Africa to collect their grievances and their demands for the proposed Freedom Charter which was adopted at Kliptown (text in Appendix). Women conducted door-to-door campaigns in the townships. This process brought forth a number of women trade union and

47

community leaders who became active especially in the ANC and the Federation of Women.

Following the Congress of the People, in December 1955, the Government retaliated by arresting 156 persons active in the anti-apartheid movement, including 22 women, and charged them with treason. Indian and African women organized a feeding and washing system for the prisoners, and the Treason Trial Defense Fund was set up to provide for the needs of the families left with only one or no parents. By 1961 all the charges had been dropped or the accused found not guilty, but the defendants' lives had been totally disrupted.

C. Individual Women in the Anti-Apartheid Movement

With the election of the "purified" National Party to power in 1948 the organizations and individuals opposed to apartheid began to move closer together around the common goal of eliminating white supremacy. The political arguments and power intrigues were minimized in the recognition that the National Party intended to control everyone by whatevery means necessary, and the first step was to label every opponent a "communist."

The first major anti-apartheid campaign in the fifties was the ANC's 1952 Defiance Campaign, followed by the Congress of the People in 1955. Several African, Indian, and Colored women leaders participated in both activities, including Ida Mntwana, Annie Silinga, Lilian Ngoyi, Florence Matomela, Ms. Ngongwe, Fatima Meer, and Ms. Singh. Speakers at an April 6, 1952, Defiance Campaign rally in Cape Town included Cissie Gool and Ms. F. Thaele. A few whites participated in the Defiance Campaign by entering African townships without permits - two women, Freda Troupe and Bettie du Toit; and two men, Patrick Duncan and Albie Sachs.

Many of these same women organized the protests against Bantu Education and extension of the passes to women, and participated in the formation in 1954 of the Federation of South African Women.

Ray Alexander of the Food and Canning Workers Union called the organizing conference of the Federation, which included as participants Hilda Watts Bernstein, Fatima Meer, Lilian Ngoyi and Helen Joseph. The latter two became officers and then leaders of the massive march on Pretoria in 1956.

The Government's reaction to this increasing opposition is best exemplified by the arrests late in 1955 and the charges of treason made against 156 leaders of the Congress Movement including the following women:

Yetta Barenblatt	European secretary and trade unionist.
Helen Joseph	English secretary of a Johannesburg medical aid society Organizer of the Federation of South African Women and its anti-pass movement. Member of the National Executive of the COD.
Bertha Mashaba	African typist. Organizer for the ANC Women's League.
Ida Mntwana	African dressmaker. President of the Transvaal

	and the National ANC Women's League, from 1948 - 1955.
Lilian Ngoyi	African garment worker. President of the National ANC Women's League from 1955-1960. Member, ANC National Executive Committee and President, Federation of South African Women. Leader of anti-pass campaigns.
Mary Ranta	African machinist. Union organizer after the 1946 African Mine Workers' Union Strike.
Ruth First	European journalist for the Guardian and New Age. Editor of the monthly Fighting Talk. (All Communist Party publications.)
Philippa Levy	Member of COD.
Sonia Bunting	Former executive member of Communist Party. Member of COD.
Annie Silinga	African trade unionist and ANC Women's League leader.
Frances Baard	African teacher and trade unionist. Leader of ANC Women's League, Eastern Cape.
Stella Damons	Colored trade unionist. Organized protests against race classification.
Christina Jasson	Colored clerk. Trade union organizer in Port Elizabeth.
Florence Matomela	African organizer in the Cape Province (imprisoned six weeks during the Defiance Campaign). Active in SACTU.
Jacqueline Arenstein	European journalist. Former Durban correspondent of the Guardian. Member of the COD.
Bertha Mkize	African teacher. Leader in anti-pass campaigns from 1931 on.
Dorothy Nyembe	ANC Women's League Organizer (imprisoned two times during the Defiance Campaign).
Dorothy Shanley	European nursery school teacher in Durban. Active with trade union organizing.
Martha Mohlakoane	African domestic servant. Active in the ANC since 1939.
July Mashaba	African factory worker. Active in the Defiance Campaign.

Zainap Asvat, an Indian woman doctor, who herself had been active in the Indian Passive Resistance in the forties, organized a food program to provide the prisoners with two hot meals per day for the first sixteen days. All the food was donated by non-European shopkeepers and white businesses and wholesalers. Bettie du Toit was actively involved in obtaining these donations. African women did the washing for the prisoners daily. Ellen Hellman of the SAIRR was the only woman among the four persons who set up and became trustees of the Treason Trial Defense Fund which helped provide legal defense for the prisoners and assistance for their families. In several cases both parents had been arrested.

Some key "anti-apartheid" women missing from the Congress Movement and the Congress of the People were the Garment Workers' Union leaders and Margaret Ballinger, the one woman Natives'

Representative in Parliament and the Chair of the new Liberal Party. The Liberal Party, though invited, declined to participate in the Congress of the People.

Many leaders of trade unions had already been removed from office through bannings under the Suppression of Communism Act. These leaders were not part of the Treason Trials, though most were close friends and associates of the accused. By September 1953 the Minister of Justice had removed thirty-three trade union officials from office and prohibited them from attending gatherings. These included the following women:

R.H. Fleet	South African Hairdressers' Employees' Union
Joey Fourie	South African Hairdressers' Employees' Union
Bettie du Toit	National Union of Laundering, Cleaning, and Dyeing Workers
Ray Alexander	First General Secretary of the Food and Canning Workers' Union
Haidee le Roux	Sweet Workers' Union
J. Wolfson	Jewelers' and Goldsmiths' Union
Nancy Dick	Textile Workers' Industrial Union (Cape)

Women trade union leaders banned later in the fifties included:

Rebecca Lan	General Secretary of the Cape Food and Canning Workers' Union
Sarah Wentzel	General Secretary of the Cape Food and Canning Workers' Union
Ronnie Press	General Secretary of the Textile Workers' Industrial Union
Phyllis Altman	Member of the National Executive Committee of SACTU
Mildred Lesiea	Cape Food and Canning Workers' Union
Elizabeth Mafekeng	Cape Food and Canning Workers' Union (fought for recognition of African unions in the Cape)
Leslie Messina	General Secretary of SACTU

Other women banned during the fifties included some Treason Trial defendants and active members of the Congress Alliance:

Ruth First	Treason Trial. New Age reporter.
Helen Joseph	Treason Trial. Secretary, South African Federation of Women.
Sonia Bunting	Treason Trial. Active in COD.
Cissie Gool	Member, Cape Town City Council. President of the National Liberation League and the Non-European Unity Movement (1940s). Head of the Cape Franchise Action Council, which led the opposition to the removal of Colored men from the common voting rolls and called a Strike Day for May 7, 1951.
Mary Butcher Turok	Active in Defiance Campaign, COD, and the Congress of the People.

Molly Krige Fischer   Secretary of the Society for Peace and
                             Friendship with the Soviet Union.
                             Traveled to China in 1955. Former member
                             of Communist Party.
Fatima Meer   A founder of the Federation of South
                             African women. Active in SAIC.
Hilda Watts Bernstein A founder of the Federation of South African
                             Women. Former member of the Communist
                             Party Executive Committee and former member
                             of the Johannesburg City Council.

     Several of the women subjected to Government action were
active in many components of the anti-apartheid movement. Lilian
Ngoyi, for example, born in 1911 in Pretoria, became a leader of
African women during the 1952 Defiance Campaign, and in 1955
became the first woman member of the ANC National Executive
Committee since Charlotte Maxeke's unofficial membership between
1912 and 1930. She followed Ida Mntwana as President of the ANC
Women's League, serving from 1955 until the ANC was banned in 1960.
Ngoyi also served on the Transvaal Executive of the ANC.
     During the Defiance Campaign Ngoyi, with four other women,
entered the European section of the Johannesburg post office and
wrote a telegram to the Minister of Justice protesting apartheid,
for which she was arrested. In 1954 she led the ANC opposition
to the Bantu Education Act, and in 1955 and 1956 the Federation
opposition to the extension of the pass to women.
     Ms. Ngoyi, trained as a nurse, became a machinist in an
Austrian women's blouse factory in 1945 and an official of the
Garment Workers' Union Native Branch. She had grown up in a
Methodist family and came to oppose the church for its inability
or unwillingness to help the poor. As a worker and trade union
member she learned the strength of organization and united action.
In May of 1952 she participated in the garment workers meeting in
Johannesburg protesting the banning of the general secretary, E.S.
Sachs, which was broken up by the police by force. And in 1954
she was elected to the Executive Committee of the GWU.
     As a representative of the ANC she participated in the 1954
national conference of women at which the Federation of Women was
formed, and was elected National Vice-President as well as President
of the Transvaal branch. She became President of the Federation
in 1956. In 1955 the Federation sent her and Dora Tamane as
delegates to the World Congress of Mothers held in Switzerland by
the Women's International Democratic Federation, to which the S.A.
Federation was affiliated. As part of the trip the women visited
China, the USSR, East Germany, and England - all without South
African passports.
     In 1956 Ms. Ngoyi became one of the Treason Trial defendants,
and was not acquitted until the end of the trial in 1961. Perhaps
the best measure of the degree of her involvement in the anti-
apartheid movement is the banning order she received in 1961
prohibiting her from attending any gatherings and restricting her
to Orlando township. By the ban she was forced to leave her job
and to earn her living as a dressmaker in Orlando. The ban was

finally lifted in 1973, after Ms. Ngoyi had been restricted to Orlando for 4,018 days, just over 11 years. When the banning order was lifted Ms. Ngoyi stated in an interview

> ' It has been quite a strain but I willed myself to stick it out. I wish my mother, who died in 1970, was still alive to share my happiness. Through many years she was the pillar of my strength...I had to give up my trade union job and do dressmaking at home but the S.B. (Security Branch) scared my customers away. They would come in at all times and start asking for passes and asking a lot of questions. So, many people decided to keep away from my place. I must say I have had a tough time, but my spirits have not been dampened...

> ' If I had the money I would buy a tourist ticket and travel all over my beautiful country and see all the things and people I have been missing for 11 years." (Sechaba, volume 7, nos. 10/11/12; October/November/December 1973; page 26; an interview reprinted from Drum)

Later that same year Lilian Ngoyi was detained in solitary confinement for 71 days, an experience which she called her worst. In another interview with Drum she stated

> ' While detained my health deteriorated so much that one day I fainted. I just collapsed. For a moment I thought that the end had come, but somehow I pulled through...I just pray that I be left in peace now,' (page 27)

Another woman leader in the anti-apartheid movement, Helen Fennell Joseph, born in 1905 in Sussex, England, an Anglican, moved to South Africa in 1931. In 1939 she became an "honorary organizer" for the Indian Women's Club in Durban and following the War worked with various community centers. In 1951 Ms. Joseph became Secretary of the Transvaal Clothing Industry Medical Aid Society, the largest benefit society in South Africa (21,000 members). She joined the Labor Party in 1952 and in 1953 helped form the Congress of Democrats, serving as the first secretary of the Hillbrow Branch in Johannesburg, and as Vice President on the first national executive committee. Also in 1953 Ms. Joseph became one of the Transvaal representatives to the South Africa Peace Council, and was active with Lilian Ngoyi in the National Education Movement which established the cultural clubs for Africans, to counter Bantu Education.

When the Federation of South African Women was formed in 1954, Helen Joseph became the first general secretary. She helped organize the Congress of the People for June 1955 and in October helped with the Transvaal Branch of the Federation protest against the pass laws, in which nearly 2,000 African women participated. Then in December she was arrested and charged with treason. Despite this, she and Lilian Ngoyi, also a Treason Trial defendant, led the Federation's massive 1956 anti-pass campaigns.

Although banned in 1957 Ms. Joseph could attend political and anti-apartheid meetings until she was placed under house arrest on the 13th of October in 1962. Under the house arrest Ms. Joseph was allowed out of her house for twelve hours a day on weekdays (6 AM to 6 PM), was required to report to a police station one time per day, and could not attend any gathering of three or more persons. The ban was finally lifted following world-wide protests after she was hospitalized for cancer in 1973. While under house arrest Helen Joseph found an explosive device on her front gate, received anonymous phone calls and death threats, found her house advertized for sale, and had several tons of top soil delivered to her home. Such harrassment is particularly difficult to bear when you cannot go to friends, seek assistance from the police, or just have friends come to stay with you.

Another woman leader was Annie Silinga, born in the Transkei in 1910, and a resident of Langa township near Cape Town beginning in 1937. Ms. Silinga joined the Langa Branch of the ANC in 1952 and participated in the Defiance Campaign. As a result she spent two weeks in jail with her six-month old baby. Then in 1954 she led the women's anti-pass campaign in the Western Cape. In 1955 she was arrested again, for refusing to accept a pass, and was finally convicted and deported to Namaqualand in the Transkei in 1956. Having defied the deportation order and remained in Langa, she was arrested again, freed, and then caught in the raids prior to the Treason Trials. She was among the Treason Trial defendants the charges against whom were dropped in 1957. Then in 1958 she was elected president of the Cape Town ANC Women's League.

Margaret Gazo from Springs was active in the ANC and the Transvaal branch of the Federation of Women. She organized the October 1955 anti-pass demonstration of 2000 African women.

Florence Matomela, a Treason Trial defendant, had helped found the revived ANC Women's League in the Eastern Cape. She served as a leader of the Food and Canning Workers' Union in the Eastern Cape, and was held in solitary confinement in 1963. She died in 1969 on release from a five-year term in prison for membership in the ANC. Her death was caused by not being given insulin regularly while in prison.

Frances Baard, a Treason Trial defendant and a former domestic servant and teacher, served as secretary of the Port Elizabeth ANC Women's League from 1950 on. She helped organize the Eastern Cape Food and Canning Workers' Union and SACTU. She was imprisoned in the sixties for ANC membership and activity.

Ray Alexander, founder of the Federation of Women, organized the Food and Canning Workers' Union and became the Union's general secretary. Even though removed by the Government from trade union office in 1953, she was elected as a Natives' Representative to Parliament in 1954, but the Government refused to allow her to be seated.

Florence Mophosho organized the Alexandra ANC Women's League and served as Branch Secretary, and in 1956 organized the Alexandra bus boycott. (During the boycott she organized meetings every evening and pickets for every morning). (As an exile she became the African Secretary in the Women's International Democratic Federation in the German Democratic Republic.)

Dr. Margaret Mncadi was Medical director of St. Cyprian's Hospital in Sophiatown. She served as Vice President of the ANC Women's League and as a member of the Executive Committee of the Natal ANC. Dr. Mncadi in the late fifties tried to organize the women participating in the rural riots in Natal.

Sonia Beryl Bunting joined the Communist Party in 1941 at the age of 18 and was a founding member of the COD in 1953, secretary of the Cape Town Peace Council, and an organizer of the Congress of the People in 1955.

Ruth First Slovo also joined the Communist Party in the forties while a student at the University of the Witwatersrand. In 1946 she served as Acting Secretary of the Party when the Executive Committee was arrested. She worked as Johannesburg editor of the Guardian, Transvaal editor of New Age, and editor of Fighting Talk, through which she exposed floggings of farm laborers, farm prisons, and shootings following rural protest movements. She also was a founder of the COD in 1953.

Bertha Mkize led the participation of Durban women in the Federation of Women's anti-pass campaigns, and Ms. Nongwe, Port Elizabeth women. Rahima Moosa and Sophie Williams led the Indian and oriental participants in the Federation's 1956 anti-pass demonstration in Pretoria.

Though the Friends of the Soviet Union was not a popular organization or one of major impact, Mollie Krige Fischer, wife of Abram Fischer, used this organization as a way to bring together people of all races. Along with her activity in the Friends of the Soviet Union she taught Indian children, worked with the women's non-racial movement, and raised an orphaned African child along with the three Fischer children. Ms. Fischer died in an automobile accident in 1964, having been banned for nine years and detained without trial in 1960 for five months, following the "Sharpeville Massacre" and the declaration of a State of Emergency.

Mary Benson, author of The African Patriots and of a biography of Chief Lutuli, served as secretary to Michael Scott and was a founder of the Africa Bureau in London in 1952. In 1957 she became secretary of the Treason Trial Defense Fund in Johannesburg. Having participated in many aspects of the anti-apartheid movement, she had her passport confiscated by the Government in 1962, but was able to leave under a British passport.

Nadine Gordimer, the author, opposed apartheid. Through her writing she revealed the effects of apartheid to the extent that her last two books, Too Late the Bourgeous World and The Conservationist, have been banned in South Africa. Ms. Gordimer has maintained supportive friendships with many of the women who have opposed apartheid politically.

In 1955 Winnifred Mandela, a social worker; Albertina Sisulu, a nurse who had been one of the organizers of the ANC Youth League in 1944 and active in the ANC ever since; Tiny Nokwe, a teacher; and Magdalene Resha, a nurse; all local ANC Women's League leaders,

organized African women in Sophiatown and Orlando to protest the
passes. During one protest 3,000 women went to the Johannesburg
City Hall, following which 1300 women were arrested, convicted,
and sentenced. The leaders spent two weeks in prison. Freda
Matthews, President of the Cape ANC Women's League, organized
similar demonstrations there.

The Federation of Women and the ANC spurred actions by women
against the pass throughout South Africa. When officials went
to the Zeerust area to give passes to the women, they refused to
take them. Then when a police officer was sent to arrest them,
they caused him so much harrassment he ended up walking with them
and their children through the dust to Zeerust. The ANC arranged
for a Jewish woman attorney to defend the women and for Bettie du
Toit to go into the Reserve to convince witnesses they should
testify at the women's trial. People in the Reserve had been
threatened and frightened by the police, so Ms. du Toit's experience
in union organizing was needed to convince the people to take a
united stand. Ms. du Toit had to break her ban to take the trip,
enter the Reserve, and collect the witnesses.

In 1957 Chieftainess Madinoge Kholokwe of the tribe of
Sekhukhuniland in the Northern Transvaal led the opposition to
Government removals, for which she was imprisoned from 1961 through
1971, after having received a reprieve from her sentence of death.

Women held several anti-pass demonstrations as the Government
attempted again in the late fifties to extend the pass to women.
Dr. Margaret Mncadi of the Natal ANC helped rural women in Ixopo
and Umzinto to voice their grievances. They coordinated with
women's protests against the beer halls, which the Government ran
while prohibiting the township women from making their own beer,
which was a major source of income for the women. On June 18,
1959, 2,000 women from Cato Manor in Durban presented their
grievances to a local official. Police broke up the meeting with
a baton charge. The boycott and picketing of the beer halls by the
women continued, with hundreds of women being arrested.

The trade unions opposing apartheid had several women leaders
in the fifties, but these can be divided between those who broke
with the SAT&LC in 1954 and formed SACTU (which recognized
registered and African unions as equal), and those who stayed with
the re-formed SAT&LC, now called the Trade Union Council of South
Africa (TUCSA) (which incorporated a bar to African members in its
constitution).

SACTU's stated goals were to organize African workers, obtain
a national minimum wage of R2 per day, obtain trade union rights
for all workers, and eliminate the pass laws and other discriminatory legislation. Women trade union leaders who worked with SACTU
included:

Lilian Diedericks and Liz Abrahams	two of the six founding leaders of SACTU
Mabel Balfour	SACTU National Executive; Secretary, Transvaal Branch, African Food and Canning Workers' Union
Doris Telling	General Secretary of SACTU in 1955

Mary Moodley	Food and Canning Workers' Union, Transvaal
Leslie Messina	General Secretary of SACTU
Elizabeth Mafekeng	Cape Food and Canning Workers' Union
Phyllis Altmann	Assistant General Secretary of SACTU
Mildred Lesiea	Cape Food and Canning Workers' Union
Viola Hashe	Vice President of SACTU, elected to represent SACTU at the ILO but refused passport; Secretary of the National Clothing Workers' Union (African)
Frances Baard	Secretary of the African Food and Canning Workers' Union, Port Elizabeth
Nancy Dick	Textile Workers' Industrial Union
Sarah Wentzel	Cape Food and Canning Workers' Union
Rebecca Lan	Cape Food and Canning Workers' Union
Florence Matomela	
Fatima Meer	

Many of these women appeared on the list of trade union leaders banned under the SCA during the fifties.

In 1951 Dulcie Hartwell, long a leader in the Garment Workers' Union, was elected secretary of the 150,000 member South African Trades and Labor Council. When the SAT&LC and the South African Federation of Trade Unions united in 1955 to form the South African Trade Union Council, she was again elected general secretary. From this position Ms. Hartwell was responsible for the Council's organizing campaign among African unions. Ms. Hartwell was a key participant in 1953 in an attempt to obtain one coordinating body for all trade unions. The white unions opposing mixed unions and recognition of African unions ultimately prevented formation of the coordinating council. The SATUC utilized FOFATUSA and the International Confederation of Free Trade Unions to organize "anti-communist" African unions, in competition with SACTU unions. Despite remaining within the SAT&LC the GWU leaders maintained their union's mixed status and argued for recognition of African unions.

During the fifties Johanna Cornelius and Anna Scheepers of the GWU, Haidee le Roux of the Sweet Workers' Union, and Mrs. Young of the Waitresses Union, served on the National Executive Committee of the SAT&LC. In the late fifties Sarah Chitja served as Secretary-General of FOFATUSA and Lucy Mvubelo as Vice President.

In 1950 Anna Scheepers, President of the GWU since 1938, warned that passage of the Suppression of Communism Act would mean the end of trade unionism. She and the GWU were instrumental in gaining the opposition of the SAT&LC to the Bill. In 1952 she addressed the International Conference of Textile and Clothing Workers in Berlin, stating "Today the wages of clothing workers are the best of all factory workers. We are still struggling to get equal pay for men and women." (Garment Worker, volume III, no. 4, September-October 1952, p. 3) Ms. Scheepers was elected one of four Vice-Presidents of the International. Johanna Cornelius, Secretary-General of the GWU since 1953, and Katie Viljoen, Secretary of the Port Elizabeth branch of the GWU, were also to attend the conference but were refused passports.

A white trade union leader active in the ANC and the SAIC was Bettie du Toit. In the early fifties just prior to her banning from trade union activity, Ms. du Toit achieved an Industrial Conciliation Council agreement for the laundry and dry cleaning workers, which was extended to African workers, which provided for the African workers to have "observers" on the Joint Council who could participate in discussions and vote and which gave all workers a three-week vacation and an extensive benefits package. Through this agreement the African workers gained de facto trade union recognition and rights which were prohibited by law.

Following her banning Ms. du Toit set up a Cooperative Society for non-Europeans for the purchase of food. Once the program was operating in Johannesburg - in the non-European section" - she trained African women to set up their own cooperative in Orlando township. The purpose was to obtain nourishing food in quantities, wholesale, and sell it close to cost. Once she had turned the cooperative over to the African women, Ms. du Toit took a job in Orlando township under an assumed name running a school lunch program called Kupagani, "help yourself."

The Government forbade provision of free food to African children, so Ms. du Toit organized a system to provide a cup of protein soup and a slice of dark bread for one cent. She also gave nutrition classes in English to the children. Teachers, parents, the community, all helped to make the program work. Then the Security Branch discovered her, in the early sixties, and she had to flee the country to avoid long term detention and solitary confinement.

African women had several organizations in the urban African townships to help them to raise and educate their children within the constraints of the apartheid system. These included the National Council of African Women, the Orlando Mothers' Welfare Association, the Young Women's Christian Association, Zenzele, and the African Self-Help Associations. Ellen Kuzwayo in a talk given for the SAIRR on the role of women in the urban towns urged that a campaign to inform African women of their rights be initiated, that more opportunities for employment of African women be created, and that the salary differentiation between men and women be ended.

The SAIRR played a much more active role in the fifties than in the forties. Muriel Horrell directed publication of the Institute's annual Survey of Race Relations and several additional research papers on the laws of apartheid, trade unions, African workers, etc. Eleanor Hawarden led the SAIRR opposition in 1950 to the Unlawful Organizations Bill, known as the Suppression of Communism Act. Dr. Ellen Hellman, President of the Institute from 1953-1955, served as one of the four trustees of the Treason Trial Defense Fund, set up to assist the families of defendants in the 1956-1961 trials. Dr. Sheila van der Horst presented a paper on "Equal Pay for Equal Work" which served as the basis for the SAIRR's new policy endorsing equal pay for equal work, given the same education, training, experience, and responsibility.

In 1955 several white women in South Africa formed the Women's Defense of the Constitution League, which became known as the Black Sash, electing Ruth Foley as the first president. Their first major action was to oppose the packing of the Senate so the Colored male voters could be removed from the common role. However, in 1955, the Sash did not work for Colored voting rights. The women stood silent vigil outside Parliament and wherever Government ministers were traveling. The Sash did not ally itself with any anti-apartheid or multi-racial organizations in the fifties, though it did develop bases for coordination with the SAIRR.

Jean Sinclair, then a member of the Johannesburg City Council, organized the first protest. In 1960 she became president of the 2,000 member organization, followed in 1975 by her daughter, Sheena Duncan. Ms. Sinclair was quoted in the New York Times in a report of an Associated Press interview as saying

> "We thought we were going to change the history of
> South Africa...I've been in the Sash from its first
> day and now it's my life...Our work is ineffectual
> ...We try and help these people in the clutches of
> this cruel legislation, but we have little success.
> Occasionally we get a lawyer to appeal on a case,
> but the costs are high, the bureaucracy effective
> and the chance of success slim.

> "We keep on the work and help these poor people
> understand what is being done to them. The advice
> bureau is full every day.

> "The misery and suffering is heartbreaking. To
> see a woman with a baby at her breast sobbing
> because she and her husband have to part...I could
> not live and not try to help her." (NYT 30.8.71, p. 24)

A number of the women who had been active as political candidates for the Communist Party were banned or exiled in the early fifties. Ray Alexander, though banned from trade union activity, ran for Natives' Representative of Cape Western in 1954, after first Sam Kahn (in 1952) and then Brian Bunting (1953) had been elected and unseated by the National and United Party MPs. Ms. Alexander in turn won the election, by a 2500 vote majority, but was not allowed to be seated. Margaret Ballinger, a Natives' Representative in Parliament throughout the fifties, opposed the banning of the three elected Representatives as an attempt to deprive Africans of their only means of participation in the Parliament. No further election was held, thus leaving the seat vacant until all Natives' Representatives' seats were abolished in 1960. Ms. Ballinger did not support the ANC boycott of Bantu Education nor did she participate in the Congress Alliance or the Congress of the People.

Helen Suzman was elected to Parliament in 1953, as a United Party candidate. She was one of twelve MPs who broke from the UP in 1959 to form the Progressive Party which stood for a qualified franchise. (In 1963 she was the only MP of the twelve who was re-elected, leaving her the sole MP from the Progressive Party.)

Bertha Solomon, a member of Parliament and of the Executive

Council of the SAIRR in the fifties, and an advocate, led a lonely fight for the equality of all women under South African law.

Cissie Gool served as the representative of Ward 6 (the Colored area in Cape Town) on the Cape Town City Council from 1938-1954, when she was banned under the SCA.

Katie Gelvan, secretary of the Garment Workers' Union Port Elizabeth branch from 1938 on, was elected to the Walmer Ward City Council as an independent. She held the seat for several years, being returned unopposed in 1958. During the fifties she chaired the Council's housing committee, and was honored by having one of the Council's housing schemes named "Gelvan Township."

Several women trade union leaders were active in the South Africa Labor Party in the fifties, including Johanna Cornelius of the GWU who served on the Executive Committee; Mrs. Holdforth, Vice Chairman of the Transvaal Provincial Executive; and Jessie McPherson, who continued as Chairman of the SALP throughout the decade.

In the fifties women became a primary force in the anti-apartheid movement, but only through their own organizations – and South African Federation of Women, the ANC Women's League, and the predominantly female unions – and through individual actions and associations. Within the other anti-apartheid organizations women still had relatively minor official roles, except in the trade union councils – the SAT&LC (later the SATUC), FOFATUSA, and SACTU. The women organized and ran anti-apartheid actions and campaigns, but they were not recognized as leaders except within some sections of the trade union movement. In this respect the anti-apartheid organizations followed the example of the political, social, and industrial structure of white South Africa.

The fifties show again the leadership of the women in the anti-apartheid events, but the people officially recognized as leaders and spokespersons were still the men. The women, however, did have enough impact to cause the Government to arrest, imprison, and ban them. And the extension of the pass to women was held off for another decade.

CHAPTER 7

VII. THE SIXTIES

During the 1950s the Government crushed passive resistance organizations and efforts to change the apartheid laws and police state tactics of the South African Government. Leaders of anti-apartheid organizations and demonstrations were banished and banned. Newspapers and organizations were banned. Non-whites were increasingly restricted in their movements. Fewer and fewer opportunities existed for people of different races to meet. And 156 leaders of the anti-apartheid movement were arrested, imprisoned, and put through a one to four year trial, the end result of which was dismissal of the charges or finding of not-guilty by the courts. The Government was determined to find means to control people opposed to Government policy.

Then in March 1960 the ANC plan to hold an anti-pass campaign was pre-empted by the Pan African Congress (PAC) march on police stations by Africans who, having left their passes at home, demanded to be arrested as passive resisters to the pass laws. In Sharpeville and Langa townships the police opened fire, killed 69 Africans, and wounded 178. Prime Minister Verwoerd declared a State of Emergency, banned the ANC and the PAC, the only functioning African national organizations, and arrested and detained over 10,000 people. Both organizations immediately went underground. Parliament voted to abolish the seats for Natives' Representatives. And a major uprising in Pondoland was crushed by force.

Then in 1961 the Union of South Africa proclaimed its independence from Britain, becoming the Republic of South Africa. The underground ANC announced formation of Umkhonto we Sizwe (Spear of the Nation), formed to commit acts of sabotage. The ANC had moved from a policy of non-violence to sabotage, as the only way left to oppose the apartheid Government of South Africa.

The Government responded to anti-apartheid pressure and action with further restrictive legislation:

1960   Unlawful Organizations Act. Gave the Governor General
            the authority to declare the PAC and the ANC, and
            similar organizations, to be unlawful organizations.
            (The Congress of Democrats was suppressed under this
            Act in September 1962.)
1961   General Law Amendment Act. Provided for twelve-day
            detention without charge. Made it an offense to
            encourage holding as well as to actually convene or
            address a meeting banned under the Riotous Assemblies
            Act.
1962   General Law Amendment Act. Created the offense of sabot-
            age, providing for a minimum sentence of five years.
            Expanded banning restrictions and provided for house
            arrest.

1963	Transkei Constitution Act. Established citizenship and a legislative assembly for the Transkei.
1963 & 1964	Bantu Laws Amendment Acts. Increased influx control and transferred local officials' influx powers to "labor bureaux." Established aid centers.
1963	Better Administration of Designated Areas Act. Provided for the removal of Alexandra township near Johannesburg.
1963	General Law Amendment Act. Provided for 90-day detention without charge or trial.
1965	Criminal Procedure Amendment Act. Provided for 180-day detention without charge or trial.
1965 a.	Government Notice 1308. Prohibited Colored teachers from being members of the National, United, Progressive, or Liberal Parties.
b.	Government Notice 1375. Made it an offense to hold or to address a gathering of more than five persons in rural Colored areas.
1965	Bantu Homelands Development Corporations Act. Provided for establishment of a development corporation in each African homeland, using whites for all management positions.
1966	Bantu Laws Amendment Act. Provided that only "citizens" of a self-governed Bantu territory (Homeland) can enter or live in that territory.
1967	Terrorism Act. Created the crime of terrorism with a minimum sentence of five years in prison. Provided for indefinite detention without trial of suspected "terrorists." (Retroactive to 1962) The burden of proof is on the accused.
1968	Prohibition of Political Interference Act. Prohibited multi-racial political parties and meetings.

In 1969 the Security Branch became the Bureau of the State Security (BOSS) which was given the power to control the entry of evidence to the courts, based on relevance to "state security."

In 1963 the Government spy and informer system led the Security Branch to the headquarters of the underground ANC and the South African Communist Party (SACP) which resulted in the arrest of ten leaders. The consequent "Rivonia Trial" and sentencing deprived the ANC and the SACP of much of the underground structure and leadership which had been developed. Abram Fischer, of a leading Afrikaner family, led the defense at the trial and later himself was arrested, tried, and imprisoned for life as a communist and a leader of violent efforts to overthrow the South African Government.

As the lines became more clearly drawn between those "for" and "against" the Government, as defined by the Government, the South African economy boomed. Expansion of industry necessitated expansion of the skilled labor force and industrial color bars began to crack. But the Government passed legislation to encourage border industries near the Homelands/Reserves, to develop towns - housing, schools, small businesses, and recreational areas - within the Reserves but near the factories, to form Bantu Investment Corporations, and to establish functional Bantu governments in the

Reserves。 Africans, Coloreds, and Indians were removed to areas
set aside for members of their race, and separate educational and
governmental systems were mandated. This was the Government's
first concentrated effort to implement apartheid in its ideological
form。

In 1964 the Minister of Bantu Administration stated in
Parliament that 464,726 Africans had been endorsed out of the 23
major towns between 1956 and 1963. In 1964, 85,000 men and 15,000
women were officially reported to have been endorsed out of the
nine main urban areas; in 1965, 66,303 men and 19,883 women. · (The
Minister would not release further statistics.) The Black Sash
reported that in October 1967 in Langa Township near Cape Town the
ratio of men to women was 10:1. Out of the population of 33,000,
25,000 were men living in bachelor barracks, 68 percent of whom
were married and forced to live apart from their families.

By the late sixties many Africans had no legal right to live
anywhere in South Africa, the land of their birth. By 1967 the
Government had set up 24 camps in the Reserves housing 49,000 of
these "displaced" Africans. By 1968 there were 31 such camps, all
described as having intolerable living conditions.

Still the population of South Africa continued to increase
throughout the sixties:

	1960	Percent	1967	Percent
African	10,907,789	68.2	12,750,000	68.1
Colored	1,509,258	9.4	1,859,000	9.9
Asian	477,125	3.0	561,000	3.0
White	3,088,492	19.3	3,563,000	19.0

By 1960, 29 percent of the Africans, 62 percent of the Coloreds,
and 80 percent of the Asians lived in urban areas, a total of
4,509,123 people, as compared to 2,461,162 whites.

The only legitimate power base remaining for blacks in the
urban areas in the 1960s was the trade union, even though African
unions could not be registered. A number of employers had found
that when the workers were organized, it was much easier to deal
with them, and that this was the only way the rapidly rising
number of wildcat strikes could be contained。 During the 1960s
both TUCSA and SACTU committed staff and funds to organize African
workers。 All the unions, including the Afrikaner - dominated
federations, had come to realize that as workers and as unions
they had no power by themselves. But the unions still could not
agree on admitting Africans as members. ·When the TUCSA decided in
1968 to expand membership to African workers, it lost 14 union
affiliates。 So then in 1969 TUCSA reversed its position again and
excluded African unions。

In 1961, 31.7 percent of the economically active white population were members of trade unions, 19。2 percent of the Colored
and Asian, and only 2 percent of the African。 Only 10 percent of
the mineworkers belonged to unions. By 1968 only 30.3 percent of
the economically active white population, 16 percent of the Colored,
21.2 percent of the Asian and 0.3 percent of the African, were
members of trade unions. (RR 9.69. Horrell) Only 24 works

62

committees, the Government's alternative to recognition of African trade unions, existed in South African factories, leaving the majority of African workers with no legal means of communicating with employers.

The trade unions continued in the sixties to be affiliated with four main federations:

Trade Union Congress of South Africa - 191,063 (1965) 22 percent
    non-white, including 2,012 Africans
South African Confederation of Labor - 189,500 Afrikaners (1965)
SACTU - 53,323 (including 38,791 Africans)
FOFATUSA (disbanded in 1966) - 13,000 Africans (an ICTFU affiliate)

The total number of registered trade union members in South Africa at the end of 1963 included 344,752 whites, 90,143 Coloreds, and 31,739 Asians. Yet approximately 2.4 million Africans and 1 million whites worked in the urban areas alone.

In 1960 the total Gross Domestic Product had a value of 4,812.6 million Rand, 12.2 percent of which came from agriculture, 13.6 percent from mining, 13.1 percent from commerce, and 19 percent from manufacturing. By 1966 the GDP had nearly doubled, increasing to 7,922.0 million Rand, with only 10.3 percent coming from agriculture, 12.2 percent from mining, 13.6 percent from commerce, and 21.7 percent from manufacturing.

During the sixties the National Party increased the number of seats it held in the House of Assembly from 102 to 126 (including an increase of ten in the number of seats in Parliament), and in 1966 they received 58.6 percent of the vote. In 1968 the Liberal Party dissolved itself upon passage of the Prohibition of Improper Interference Act which made it an offense for a person of one race to be a member of or take part in the activities of an organization of another race when such organization was of a political nature. The Liberal Party upon dissolution had 3,000 members, 1500 of whom were black. The task of calling the Government to account in its treatment of blacks then fell to the Progressive Party and its sole member in Parliament.

The South African Labor Party adopted a platform in 1961 calling for abolition of the pass laws; improvement of educational, occupational, health, and housing facilities for Africans; and abolition of the migrant labor system. But they had no Members of Parliament.

In 1968 Parliament established the South African Indian Council, to consist of 25 members plus a five-member executive committee. This Council replaced the temporary National Indian Council set up by the Government in 1963 to counter the activist South African Indian Congress.

In 1966 Prime Minister Verwoerd was assassinated by a deranged white man, and John Vorster was elected by the National Party to succeed him.

A major change in Government budget priorities occurred in the sixties with Defense expenditures increasing from 43.6 million Rand in 1960-61 to 157 in 1963-64; and Police expenditures from 18.1 million Rand in 1960-61 to 25.4 in 1963-64. (van den Berghe, p. 308)

A. Anti-Apartheid Events

1960	Anti-Pass Demonstrations followed by the "Sharpeville Massacre" and the State of Emergency.
1960	Banning of the PAC and the ANC.
1960	Pondoland uprising. Anti-pass and anti-Bantu Authority demonstrations.
25.3.61	All-In African Conference in Pietermaritzburg, attended by over 1000 delegates. Demanded a People's Convention in May to coincide with declaration of the Republic.
29-30.5.61	African General Strike with 10-15 percent of African workers striking except on the Witwatersrand where 40 percent were out.
1961	Announcement of formation of <u>Umkhonto we Sizwe</u> (Spear of the Nation) by the ANC.
1961	Formation of the African Resistance Movement and the National Committee for Liberation which set up training programs for guerilla warfare.
1961	Bus Boycott in Port Elizabeth.
1962	Congress of Democrats banned.
1962	Poqo - murder of whites in the Cape and Paarl.
1963, 1965, 1967	Protests against the General Law Amendment Acts which provided for detention without charge and without trial.
1963-64	Rivonia arrests and trials.
1964-65	Trials of Abram Fischer, et alia.
1966	Defence and Aid banned in South Africa.
1968	Liberal Party dissolved.
1968	Formation of the Christian Institute's Study Project on Christianity in Apartheid Society (SPRO-CAS)
1969	Colored electorate voted in 26 Labor Party (anti-apartheid) candidates to the Colored Representative Council. Pro-Government candidates won 14 seats, but the Government nominated its own 20 candidates to obtain a majority on the Council.

B. The Role of Women in Anti-Apartheid Organizations Trade Unions

In the sixties as in the fifties the role of white, Colored, and African women in the trade union movement leadership was effectively diminished by the Government through bannings and house arrests. The entire leadership of SACTU was decimated by these Government actions. TUSCA did not have many new women trade union leaders. But in the African unions women played a major role. Nearly half of the African unions in the late sixties had a woman general secretary.

Political Parties. Women served in the leadership of the Liberal Party, until its dissolution in 1968, and of the Progressive Party. The one Progressive Party MP, a woman, was the only member of Parliament to consistently question the Government on removals, bannings, house arrests, pass arrests, prison conditions, and other effects of apartheid legislation.

The SACP, underground, apparently continued to have a few women on the Executive Committee, and recruited women for the new underground organizational structure within South Africa. Communist Party activities became so closely intertwined with the ANC and Umkhonto we Sizwe that the role of women in each cannot be distinguished through public documents.

Non-white National Organizations. The ANC became closely aligned with the SACP in the sixties, and began training guerillas. Women were accepted for the military/guerilla training but initially were kept in the "rear guard." Women worked, especially inside South Africa, to recruit and organize, and to provide escape routes and channels of communication. A number of women served prison terms for membership and participation in the ANC.

The PAC was more male-dominated than the ANC - not even having a "Women's League." A breakaway group of PAC (apparently all male) formed Pogo in the Western Cape in the early sixties and carried out numerous acts of violence against Africans who cooperated with the Government or who opposed Pogo, and against whites living in the rural areas. Three Colored women were murdered, reportedly for causing men to stay away from Pogo meetings.

In 1969 black students broke from NUSAS and formed the South African Students Organization (SASO). These students based their activities on a philosophy of black consciousness, symbolized by their slogan, "I am oppressed and therefore Black." Women had no leadership role in the organization, although a few women were active members.

Interracial Organizations. In the 1960s the SAIRR became more involved in special projects to change the effects of apartheid legislation. SAIRR joined with the Black Sash, which became more clearly an anti-apartheid organization in the sixties, to set up advice centers for Africans in urban areas. These centers were staffed completely by women. Women continued to be integrally involved in the research and publication components of the SAIRR. In addition, in 1969, the Natal Region of the SAIRR organized art classes for African children in the Lamontville Municipal Township during the July school vacation. Women teachers and secondary students ran the program.

Individual church leaders opposed the removal of Africans, assisted political detainees in obtaining trials and defense attorneys, and continued to hold multi-racial meetings. All opposed the ANC/SACP sabotage campaign, but many took the position that violence was inevitable given the Government's actions. These church "leaders" were all men, but many individual women and women's church organizations took action on their own to alleviate the effects of apartheid.

The churches still excluded women from their leadership and encouraged their female members to participate in social welfare projects. The Christian Institute, however, the leading anti-apartheid organization among the churches of South Africa, involved a few women in the Study Project on Christianity in Apartheid Society, (SPROCAS) both on staff and on study commissions.

With the banning of its leaders, both black and white, the Federation of South African Women gradually died during the sixties, though its members continued to participate in anti-apartheid campaigns inside and outside South Africa.

Members of the Black Sash developed public education programs to inform the white population of the effects of Government action, including the pass laws, the migratory labor system, banishment of Africans, removals, urban area population controls, detention without trial, etc. The Black Sash also organized demonstrations against the 90-day and the 180-day detention clauses; the General Law Amendment Act of 1963; the Bantu Laws Amendment Acts of 1963 and 1964; and the declarations of African, Indian, and Colored townships or neighborhoods as white. In seeking to prevent renewal of the 90-day detention clause in 1964, the Black Sash, the National Council of Women, and the Civil Rights League formed the 90-day Detention Protest National Committee which published "Tyranny 90," presenting the case against 90-day detention. In November 1964 the Minister of Justice announced suspension of the clause as of 11 January 1965.

In the sixties the National Council of Women opposed the Sunday Sport and Entertainment Bill because it "would be completely ruinous to Non-White sporting activities." (NCW News, June 1963). A special committee of the Council investigated the unemployment situation of African children in Graaff Reinet who had completed Standard VI. They found that domestic service was the only work available to the girls. The National Council also protested the proclamation as a white area of most of District Six in Cape Town, then a Colored area.

C.   Individual Women in the Anti-Apartheid Movement

The sixties brought a dramatic change to the anti-apartheid movement: the ANC, the PAC, and the COD were banned under the Unlawful Organizations Act, and anyone guilty of furthering the aims of these organizations stood guilty of a criminal offense. The ANC and the PAC had been the only nationalist organizations through which Africans could voice their grievances and demands. (The Natives' Representatives seats in Parliament were completely abolished in 1960.) This left only the trade unions as a channel for legal expression, and even here Africans still could not be officially recognized. The ANC and the PAC re-formed underground. In 1961 came the announcement of the formation of Umkhonto we Sizwe, the military/guerrilla arm of the African nationalists:

The People's patience is not endless. The time comes in the life of any nation when there remain only two choices - submit or fight. That time has now come to South Africa.

The immediate objective was to conduct acts of sabotage to disrupt the day to day functions of the Government and the economy.

The remainder of the sixties is a story of action and counter-action, increased bannings, non-political organizations becoming the only "protesters," and new attempts by the trade unions to recognize African workers and unions and to build a trade union movement in South Africa.

The actions of the Government against individual women, including detainment, banning, banishment, and trial, provide an overall view of the role of women in the anti-apartheid movement in the sixties.

In 1960 during the State of Emergency declared following the killing of Africans by the police in Langa and Sharpeville townships during the PAC anti-pass demonstrations, several women who had been active in various anti-apartheid activities were arrested and imprisoned, including

Annie Silinga	Langa resident; Cape ANC Women's League
Sonia Bunting	SACP; COD; caught trying to escape to Bechuanaland
Bettie du Toit	Trade unionist; held in solitary for a few days
Philippa Levy	COD
Violet Weinberg	COD
Bertha Mashaba	ANC and Federation of Women
Lilian Ngoyi	ANC and Federation of Women
Helen Joseph	Federation and COD; held in solitary for a few days
Rica Hodgson	COD
Hannah Stanton	Zeerust, Warden of an Anglican Mission
Molly Drige Fischer	COD; Friends of Soviet Union
Mary Turok	SACTU
Phyllis Altman	Assistant General Secretary of SACTU

Ruth First escaped to Swaziland and then returned when the Emergency was over.

The women held in the Fort in Johannesburg demanded jointly to know the charges against them, to have better conditions, and to be allowed access to people on the outside. Several of the white women went on a hunger strike and succeeded at least in making the conditions more tolerable for both the African and the white women political prisoners. Eventually the women were removed to Pretoria where two were held in solitary for a few days, but ultimately all were released without being charged. The woman attorney who had been the women's spokesperson during their protests while in prison was detained two weeks longer than the other women.

Also in 1960 the people of Pondoland revolted against the Bantu authorities. The uprising was led by women, many of whom were arrested under the Unlawful Organizations and the Sabotage Acts. (Sechaba, 8.69)

In 1962 under new legislation the first orders for house arrest were issued by the Minister of Justice, and the first person to be so ordered was Helen Joseph, placed under 12-hour arrest on weekdays. (These orders were extended in 1966.) Within a year 24 people had been placed under such arrests, four of them women:

Sonia Bunting   24-hours
Mitta Goeiman   not publicly stated
Rica Hodgson   13-hours
and Ms. Joseph.

Both Mr. Brian P. Bunting and Mr. P.J. Hodgson had also been placed under house arrest, and those two couples, plus seven others of the 24 fled from South Africa on one-way exit permits in 1963. Rica Hodgson was accused in 1964 of being a member of the financial committee of the Communist Party and a member of Umkhonto, and of visiting the USSR. In 1964 Albertina Sisulu was also placed under house arrest, and in 1965, Ruth Hayman, an attorney active in political trials was placed under 12-hour house arrest.

Ms. Sisulu received special permission to continue working and as of October 1974 - when nearing the end of her second five-year period of banning and house arrest - held a position as nursing sister at the Johannesburg City Council's child health clinic in Orlando East. Her order allowed her out between 6 A.M. and 6 P.M. on weekdays, and 6 A.M. and 3 P.M. on Saturdays. In order to provide for her five children and the two children of her deceased sister and for their education, Ms. Sisulu also knit clothing for sale. Prior to her arrest and banning Albertina Sisulu had been a leader in the ANC Women's League and in the Federation of South African Women. (Walter Sisulu, her husband, had been sentenced to life imprisonment following the Rivonia trials.)

House arrest was a tactic used by the Smuts Government during World War II against pro-Nazi Afrikaners. The house arrest orders in the sixties, by restricting people to their homes, severely limited their means to earn a living. House arrest orders also included bans on association, prohibition of writing or publishing, and requirements to report to the local police station daily. Any association or communication with a banned person immediately drew attention from the police, which even further restricted opportunities for human association and communication. House arrest and bannings successfully silenced the active women leaders and organizers opposed to apartheid.

In November 1962 Diana Schoon, Anne Nicholson, and Molly Anderson were warned by a chief magistrate that if they did not end their political activities, they would be placed under house arrest. Eventually they and several other women received banning orders which for the trade unionists included a prohibition from holding any union office:

Jacqueline Arenstein   SACP
Winnie Mandela   ANC
Gillian E. Jewell   Sabotage
Sarah B. Brown   SACP
Mildred Lesiea   SACTU; secretary of Brick, Cement and Quarry
                           Workers' Union
Viola Hashe   Vice President of SACTU; secretary of the
                           National Clothing Workers' Union
Mabel Balfour   National Executive Committee of SACTU;

	secretary, Transvaal Branch, African Food and Canning Workers' Union
Mary Moodley	SACTU Organizer, Transvaal Branch, African Food and Canning Workers' Union
Frances Baard	SACTU; Secretary, Port Elizabeth Branch, African Food and Canning Workers' Union
Amy Rietstein	SACP
Shantie Naidoo	SAIC and SACTU
Mollie Krige Fischer	SACP
Gillian Gane	Student
Ruth Hayman	Attorney; Liberal Party; involved in political trials
Heather Morkill	Secretary, Pietermaritzburg Branch of Liberal Party
Mary Benson	Author working with Michael Scott

Elizabeth Mafekeng of the Cape Food and Canning Workers' Union was banished in 1963 from Paarl to a farm in the Northern Cape, but escaped to Basutoland. Viola Hashe was confined to the magisterial district of Roodepoort in 1964, and so was forced to give up the union position she had held for 17 years. Phyllis Altman had to resign her SACTU position, and could not find another job because of employers' fear of hiring a banned person. Molly Doyle, secretary of SACTU, was arrested and imprisoned (1965).

Between 1963 and 1965 the Government initiated several legal actions against people still active in banned anti-apartheid organizations. A number of women were charged under the Suppression of Communism Act, the Unlawful Organizations Act, and the Sabotage Act.

Florence Matomela, for example, was held in 1963 under 90-day detention, and then was sentenced to five years in prison for being a member of the ANC. When she was released from prison, she was taken back to the Eastern Cape to face further charges. A friend who visited her there told her her husband and sister had both died while she was in prison. While in solitary confinement, Ms. Matomela had not received insulin regularly, so that even though acquitted of the further charges shortly after her release from prison, she died. She had been active in the Defiance Campaign, a Treason Trial defendant, and a trade union and ANC Women's League leader in the Eastern Cape.

Dorothy Nyembe was arrested in 1963, tried, and sentenced to three years in prison, for leading the "Natal Women's Revolt" in Natal, during which rural women refused to fill the cattle dipping tanks and actually destroyed the tanks. Born in 1930 Ms. Nyembe had been active for years in the ANC Women's League, serving as leader of the Natal contingent in the 1956 anti-pass demonstration in Pretoria, vice-chair of the Durban branch, and their national president (1959). In 1960 she organized the Anti-Pass Women's Committee in Durban, and was elected chair. Then in 1962 she was elected chair of the Natal Rural Areas Committee. It was this Committee which organized the "Natal Women's Revolt" and developed a rural underground network for the ANC. Following her release from prison in 1966 Ms. Nyembe was served with banning orders and restricted to Durban. Then in 1968 she was arrested, held in solitary, and finally tried on five counts under the SCA. Found guilty (along with 11 men) of harboring terrorists and attempting to establish guerilla bases, she was sentenced to 15 years in prison (Barberton) in 1969.

Joyce Mapolisa, a domestic servant in Port Elizabeth, was one of five women and 34 men sentenced to prison in 1963 for sabotage. Following her release after six years in prison, Ms. Mapolisa was banished with her three children to Dimbaza. There she contracted tuberculosis and suffered from malnutrition. (Sechaba, May 1974)

In 1963 a British woman, Bridget Mellor, was told to leave South Africa because she helped an African to escape to Bechuanaland. Ms. Gillian Gane, a student at the University of Rhodes, left South Africa in 1964 during the round-up of suspected members of the African Resistance Movement.

Early in 1964 the Alexander Trial in Cape Town found several women guilty under the Sabotage Act, including trade union leader Mildred Lesiea, who was sentenced to three years in prison. For the first year of imprisonment the women were kept in solitary confinement in Kroonstad Prison. Later they moved along with other African women convicted of membership in and active support of banned organizations to Nelspruit in the Eastern Transvaal, 1,000 miles away. This move made them inaccessible to their families and friends.

Mary Moodley, a Colored trade union leader in the Transvaal, Joyce Mohamed (her daughter), and Christina Thibela (an African friend) were detained under the 90-day clause and charged in 1964 with organizing illegal escape routes and helping people to leave South Africa. All three were found guilty, fined, and given a suspended sentence. Ms. M. Singh was also detained, but received only a warning against being an accomplice to persons trying to escape from South Africa. Ms. Moodley suffered much physical pain, and bleeding hemorrhoids, during the long interrogations through-out which she was kept standing.

Rosemary Wentzel, an active member of the Black Sash in the early sixties, obtained political asylum in Swaziland. In 1964 she was kidnapped by South African police and detained under the 90-day clause, to be used as a State witness in the October 1964 African Resistance Movement (ARM) sabotage trial. She and Thelma Helmstadt were the only women out of the seven persons giving State's evidence at the trial, following 90-day detention. The State alleged in 1964 that Ms. Wentzel had been the only woman out of 18 people who first organized the National Committee for Liberation in 1962. Other women who were alleged leaders later named by the State, after they had left the country, included Mrs. R. Mutch, Mrs. A.H. Swersky, and Lorna Symington. After leaving South Africa, Ms. Symington was accused of being an accessory to a sabotage-related murder, but a Rhodesian magistrate did not grant an extradition order. Mrs. Mutch announced from Bechuanaland that she was a member of ARM.

Stephanie Kemp, a student, first held under 90-day detention, was convicted in 1964 of being a member of ARM. (The original charge of sabotage was dropped.) Ms. Kemp, along with a male

student convicted of the same charge, instituted legal action for
damages against the Minister of Justice and two members of the
Security Branch for 15 hours of continuous interrogation and
assaults which made her semi-conscious during detention prior to
trial. Ms. Kemp won a R1000 settlement out of court, which she
put in trust for the legal defense of people accused of political
crimes. She served a two-year sentence and then left South Africa
on an exit permit in 1966.

Sheila Weinberg was sentenced in 1965 to 18 months in prison
upon conviction of painting the letters "A.N.C." and the ANC emblem
on a bridge. The sentence was reduced to six months on appeal.

During 1964 over 300 men and women were arrested in Port
Elizabeth and charged with offenses under the Suppression of
Communism Act. Of these 74 were convicted of participating in
the ANC and Umkhonto.

The trials receiving the most publicity during the sixties
were those surrounding the underground leaders of the ANC and the
SACP. In July 1963 the police raided the home of Mr. and Mrs.
Arthur Goldreich in Rivonia, near Johannesburg. Several political
activists, white, Indian, and African, were found there along with
documents relating to the National Liberation Movement (the underground united anti-apartheid organization) and Umkhonto we Sizwe.
No women were arrested at Rivonia. Bram Fischer served as chief
legal counsel in 1964 for the Rivonia accused. The spouses of two
defendants - Albertina Sisulu and Caroline Motsoaledi - were both
detained in 1963 for questioning about their husbands' activities.

In 1964 the police arrested Bram Fischer and charged him with
being the head of the underground anti-apartheid movement. During
the trial Mr. Fischer went into hiding, breaking his bail, and was
not found until late 1965. Violet Weinberg, Leslie Schermbrucker,
and Doreen Tucker were all held in solitary under the 180-day law
as possible witnesses for the second (1966) Fischer trial.
(Messrs. Weinberg and Schermbrucker had already been convicted of
unlawful political activity and sentenced to six years in prison.)
Ms. Weinberg was accused by the prosecution of having the key to
Mr. Fischer's hiding place in her purse when she was arrested. Ms.
Schermbrucker was accused of being a member of the Central Committee
of the SACP. She refused to give evidence at the Fischer trial
and was sentenced to 300 days in prison. Both women were later
placed under house arrest.

Doreen Tucker, a former member of the COD and organizer of
the Congress of the People in 1955, gave evidence at the Fischer
trial, after being held 180-days in solitary confinement, and then
upon her release was "listed" as a communist, in July of 1966.
Ms. Tucker had been accused of passing money from various sources
- including the Communist Party - to the ANC while she was the
Johannesburg administrator of the Defense and Aid Fund, which
provided financial and legal assistance to political prisoners
and their families. She left South Africa on an exit permit.

Several women were among the 12 co-defendants at the Fischer
trial:

Jean Middleton (Strachan)

Florence Duncan
Anne Nicholson
Sylvia Neame
Esther Barsel
Molly Doyle

During the trial Ms. Strachan stated she had moved from the COD and the Liberal Party to the Communist Party out of a need to actively oppose apartheid. Ms. Duncan testified that she had joined the Communist Party in 1962 out of shame of being part of what the whites in South Africa were doing to non-whites. Anne Nicholson, admitting she was part of the Johannesburg branch of the CP, stated her only crime was to see that justice is done. Mr. Doyle denied being a communist, but was found guilty of participation in the SACP. Ms. Neame was sentenced to two months in prison following an attempted escape from 90-day detention and to four years in prison for CP and ANC activity, but was released in 1966 upon winning her appeal to the Supreme Court.

Dr. Raymond Milindton, an elderly woman who lived near Rustenburg, was called to testify at the Fischer trial because she had provided shelter for Fischer for part of the time he was in hiding in 1964. But at the trial she stated she had not known who he was. She had been held under 180-day detention prior to the Fischer trial to give evidence for the State.

All the women convicted of political offenses were sent to Barberton Prison in the Eastern Transvaal. Following release from her three-year sentence imposed after conviction during the Fischer trial, Jean Middleton wrote about Barberton:

> I was there for three years, from 1965/68, with a
> total of eleven other white women who came and left
> at different times in a section roughly the areas
> of a moderately-sized school assembly. It was
> divided into a central space with a dining table
> and chairs and concrete laundry sinks, a courtyard
> surrounded by fifteen-foot walls and with washing
> lines in the middle, a bathroom and lavatory, three
> single cells so small that a visitor from the
> International Red Cross commented on them.
>
> Here, prisoners in Barberton prison spend their days,
> months, and years. Most prisoners work outside the
> building but they never leave it, their work is in
> their own sections and there they wash, iron, sweep
> and scrub the floors.
>
> The longest walk they take is ten yards up the cor-
> ridor to the matron's office. Scarcely do they take
> it more than twice a week. Newspapers are not allowed
> in prison, no recreation at anytime, no radio.
>
> The policy of the South African government is to try
> and 'break' the morale of political prisoners by all

means especially at the beginning of their sentences. Prisoners are allowed one hour daily exercise as prescribed in the prison regulations but the officer usually shows his power by cutting it down to as short as fifteen minutes.

It is quite certain that if white women had a bad time, the African woman is having a worse one as they are generally, according to law, treated with great contempt. According to prison regulations their food is comparatively deplorable. It consists of mainly boiled mealies without salt, and mealie-meal porridge without sugar or salt. (Sechaba, October/November/ December 1974, p. 34)

Molly Doyle, formerly secretary of SACTU, upon her release from Barberton in 1968, having served a three-year sentence, was banned and restricted for five years to her family's farm in the Ficksburg district. Although allowed to visit a village nine miles away and Ficksburg, 23 miles away, she was prohibited from visiting any African compound or factory, and from attending any social or political gatherings, or gatherings of students or pupils. She did, however, enroll in a correspondence course in library science. (Sechaba, January 1968)

Ruth First Slovo and Hilda Watts Bernstein were both accused of serving on the Central Committee of the Communist Party in the sixties, as were their husbands, and following their detention/ imprisonment, fled from South Africa via the underground. Both women had been leaders in the Communist Party prior to its going underground in 1950. (Ms. Bernstein wrote of this period in The World that Was Ours, London: Heineman, 1967). Following the Rivonia trial Bram Fischer and Ruth First had been the only members of the Communist Party Executive Committee still in South Africa and not in prison. Upon her departure Ms. First became a leader in exile in the SACP underground, and in a June 26, 1969, speech at the South Africa Freedom Day conference in London, stated that what is needed in South Africa "'is a determined leadership prepared to make great sacrifices and face the consequences of armed struggle. In South Africa sabotage in the urban areas had been an in-between stage in preparation for guerilla warfare to follow.'" (Sechaba, September 1969, pp. 16-17)

Four women were held under 180-day detention in 1965 as potential state witnesses in the trial of Fred Carneson on charges of sabotage and Communist Party activities:

Brenda Mercorio
Caroline de Crespigny
Gillian Jewell
Amy Rietstein

All four were either under or placed under banning orders following their release, and Ms. de Crespigny, a British citizen, and Ms. Jewell left South Africa. (Mr. Carneson was acquitted on the sabotage charge.)

In the trial of Isaac Heymann and Michael Dingaka in 1966 on charges of Communist Party membership and activity, Violet Weinberg and Chloe Gama were called as State witnesses, after being detained under the 180-day rule for five and six months respectively. Both refused to give evidence, and were released, following announcement that they would argue that the "statements they had made to the police, which led to their being called as witnesses, had been extracted against their will after prolonged, uninterrupted periods of interrogation." (Survey, 1966, p. 80) Both Ms. Weinberg and Ms. Gama were then brought to trial in May of 1966 at which time Ms. Gama agreed to give evidence and so the charges on refusal to testify were dropped. Ms. Weinberg testified she had been kept awake for three days of continuous interrogation, being forced to stand throughout. Having continued to refuse to give State's evidence, she was sentenced to three months in prison.

In August of 1966 Ms. Weinberg and Lesley Schermbrucker (then serving 300 days in prison for not giving evidence in the Fischer trial) were charged with participating in Communist Party activities. Both were convicted and sentenced to two years.

Other women detained under the 180-day rule were Pat Lendrum and Jean Cohen, both students, and Pooney Moodley, held as a State witness in the trial of Mooroogiah Naidoo who was indicted on seven charges under the Suppression of Communism Act.

Florence Majola, elected to the executive committee of the Federation of South African Women in 1965 and appointed secretary in 1966, received her banning order in October 1966. Though she and her family received regular attention from the police from the time of her first involvement in politics in 1960, it was not until 1969 that she began to fear total confinement. In August she was sentenced to 12 months in prison for breaking her banning order, with all but four days suspended.

> On my discharge (after serving the four days in prison)
> I began to worry about my suspended sentence and the
> police visits were intensified to the point where they
> checked on me almost daily, at home and at work. Mr.
> Swanepoel also came to try to find out why I was so
> 'anti-government,' making all kinds of offers and
> giving me names of my fellow-politicians whom he
> claimed were now free and comfortable because they
> had decided to give up their struggle. This of course
> was a police stunt. I told him I was more determined
> than ever to fight for my rights, since he had won
> others to his side. My plight became worse as pam-
> phlets would be planted in my letter box and seized
> again by the police.
>
> In December 1969, because of police harrassment I
> forgot to report to the police one Monday until 8 p.m.,
> when I would be breaking my banning order if I left
> the house. And since I knew that this fresh charge
> would bring the implementation of the suspended sentence

I decided to leave my country. On March 19th, 1970
I left and arrived in Gaberones, Botswana with my two
daughters on the same day. (Sechaba, October/November/
December 1973, p. 30)

Florence Mophosho, formerly active in the Alexandra/Johannes-
burg branch of the ANC Women's League, left South Africa in the
sixties to become the Africa Secretary of the Women's International
Democratic Federation in East Germany. Several other women who had
been active in the anti-apartheid movement in South Africa remained
in the movement after they left the country.

At the time of the trial of her husband in 1963 Winnie Mandela
had been subjected to various detainments and bannings. Then in
1969 she and 21 other persons were charged under the Terrorism Act
with furthering the aims of the ANC in Johannesburg, Durban, Port
Elizabeth, and Umtata. The charges covered organizing and
recruiting members for the ANC, arranging sabotage, giving speeches,
and propagating communist doctrine. The accused included four
women besides Ms. Mandela:

Joyce Nomafa Sikakane (reporter for the Rand Daily Mail)
Rita Anita Ndzanga
Venus Thokozile
Mhgoma Martha Dlamini

Two additional women were detained during the trial for refusing to
testify against the accused - Shantie Naidoo and Vriline Makhala.
(Shantie Naidoo had been active in the South African Indian Congress
and in SACTU until she was banned in 1963. Her brother was a
defendant in the first sabotage trial in 1963, and Ms. Naidoo had
organized opposition to the Group Areas Act in Johannesburg.)

Following withdrawal of the charges against the 22 in 1970,
all 22 were rearrested. Protests against this action, especially
by students, broke out across the country.

From the actions taken by the Government against these women
it is possible to gain some sense of the continued involvement of
women in the anti-apartheid movement and of the intense pressure
and harrassment they endured.

Several other women were active in the sixties in various
anti-apartheid efforts.

Late in 1963 a group of Indian women, led by Ms. Pillay, went
to Pretoria to convey to the Prime Minister their "lack of confi-
dence" in the Minister for Indian Affairs. Dogs were used to force
the women to disperse.

The trade unions' main step during the decade was the decision
by TUCSA to accept only bona fide trade unions as members - which
would not include African trade unions - and to request the African
union members of FOFATUSA, which dissolved in 1966, to affiliate
with TUCSA. TUCSA also adopted the policy to urge Government
recognition of African trade unions. Women played a small role
in TUCSA and the other officially recognized trade union federations in the 1960s. Only two women, Johanna Cornelius and C. du
Preez, served on the TUCSA National Management Committee, and

Dulcie Hartwell continued as general secretary of the Council.

SACTU, however, which had been hard hit by the banning and detention of its leaders, had several women officers, including Phyllis Altman who served on the National Executive Committee and as assistant general secretary until she was banned in 1964; Shantie Naidoo, banned in 1963; Miriam Sithole, acting general secretary from 1964 until she, too, was banned; Viola Hashe, Vice President; Mabel Balfour, National Executive; Mildred Lesiea, Frances Baard, and Mary Moodley.

When the President of FOFATUSA was imprisoned for activities in the Pan African Congress, the vice president, Lucy Mvubelo, and the secretary-general, Sarah Chitja, took over all the Federation's activities. Dulcie Hartwell, general secretary of TUCSA, provided extensive assistance to FOFATUSA.

Trade union leaders of the garment workers, food and canning workers, cigarette and tobacco workers, and leather and allied trades workers - all initially organized by women - maintained close liaison between the African and non-African segments of their unions when the Government forced the integrated unions to split. One of these leaders, Anna Scheepers, president of the Garment Workers' Union of South Africa, stated in an address in 1969 that the trade union movement was the only legitimate platform available to Indian and Colored workers in South Africa to air their grievances.

Many women actively opposed apartheid through more politically acceptable methods.

Jean Sinclair, president of the Black Sash throughout the sixties, moved the organization from emphasizing the South African constitution to emphasizing human rights and dignity. A major part of this change in emphasis was exhibited through the establishment of offices and advice centers in Cape Town, Johannesburg, Durban, Port Elizabeth, East London, and Elgin. In 1963 the Black Sash opened its membership to women of all races.

Helen Suzman, the only Progressive Party Member of Parliament, opposed restrictive legislation throughout the decade. She was the sole vote against the 1963 Act which included the 90-day detention clause. She voted against this Act at every stage, urging that non-whites be allowed means to address grievances. Violence would become inevitable, she stated, if the Government continued to pass such legislation. In 1963 and 1964 she opposed the Bantu Laws Amendment Acts because they would make all Africans working in urban areas migrant laborers, reducing the African in the country of his/her birth "to the level of chattel." (Survey, 1964, p. 186) Ms. Suzman also raised questions in Parliament on the numbers of political detainees, on abuses in detention, on African trade union recognition, and on prison conditions. She gained the reputation of being a one woman resistance movement, and as such was invited to visit several black African states.

Nadine Gordimer, the author, experienced the first banning of her work upon publication in 1966 of The Late Bourgeois World. Her novels portrayed the impact of apartheid on the lives of people trying to live a "normal" human existence.

The National Union of South African Students (NUSAS), which

had had very few women among its leaders, elected Margaret Marshall President in 1966. NUSAS adopted motions to urge the Government to charge or release all banned lecturers and students and to abandon Christian National Education, and they attempted to increase contact and communication among students of different races. Ms. Marshall was one of three NUSAS members who presented a petition to the Minister of Justice for the charging or release of the then President of NUSAS (1965), Ian Robertson.

In the face of massive removals and increased restrictions and controls by the Government on Africans in the urban areas, the African Self-Help Association, made up of African women, was organized. By the end of 1964 the Association had built and equipped 15 day nurseries and was running 17 others in temporary premises. Various children's feeding programs were organized by African and white women. Bettie du Toit, the banned trade union leader, ran one feeding program in Soweto and Orlando for Kupugani, providing lunch for school children and nutritional training in English - the only guise available for teaching English to the children. To do this Ms. du Toit had to break her ban. Although she had taken the job under an assumed name, the Special Branch finally discovered her, and she had to leave the country via the underground or face imprisonment.

The SAIRR became more involved in legal and social services to non-whites in the sixties. Included in the leadership were Margaret Ballinger, Hansi Pollak, Ellen Hellman, and Sheila van der Horst. The research, publications, and public education programs were maintained, especially by Muriel Horrell, but the program thrust, under the direction of members such as Anne Adams, Secretary of the Southern Transvaal Region, moved toward coordination with the Black Sash in setting up and operating advice centers, assisting with feeding schemes, and opposing removals and influx controls. Bertha Solomon, long an active member of the SAIRR and former President of the NCW and Member of Parliament, died in 1969.

In the sixties the activities of women attempting to meet the human needs of people became the heart of the internal opposition to apartheid. Political activity had been so completely suppressed that women active in political organizations which opposed apartheid, except Helen Suzman, were the subjects of bannings, house arrests, detention, trials, imprisonment, torture, and exile. Most of the women caught in this vice were either forced to become inactive or left the country.

Women of all races then took over the informal leadership of the socially-oriented, and a-political, "anti-apartheid movement." They tried to force the Government to respond to the deprivations caused to people's lives and families by Government action. And they tried to help the victims put their lives back together.

Women played a primary role in the trade union organizing among African workers in the sixties, but a minimal role in the Government-recognized trade union federations. They also began to rise to a position of stature within the underground political and military anti-apartheid movement. Generally, African women were too far removed from mainline politics and economics to even be observed or recognized by the police. Because social action was acceptable for women, the non-political activist woman was usually ignored and not viewed as a threat.

The military and violent opposition to apartheid was run by men, but the day to day opposition through resistance and refusal to comply with apartheid rules continued to be carried out by women, and mainly through women's organizations.

CHAPTER 8

VIII. THE SEVENTIES   (1970-1975)

As the rest of the world entered a period of economic decline, the South African economy continued to expand, increasing the need for laborers and skilled workers in the mines and in industry. In the early seventies Prime Minister Vorster began to implement the full policy of separate development through encouragement in the Reserves of (1) self-government, (2) economic development, (3) African-owned businesses, and (4) housing and town construction plans. In October of 1975 the paramount chief of the Transkei, Kaiser Matanzima, announced South Africa would grant independence to the Transkei on October 26, 1976. On October 7, 1975, the South African Government, business leaders, and white trade unions released a declaration stating more jobs would be open to blacks. And in November of the same year the Minister of Bantu Administration and Development, Mr. M.C. Botha, was quoted as stating

> I am particularly mindful of the need for further
> provision of a variety of the necessary ancillaries
> of civilized living which are required to relieve
> the pressures of city life. I am referring to
> amenities such as theatres, cinemas, and sports
> fields, to mention a few...A craving for these
> facilities is now indeed strongly discernible and
> has to be met. The need, therefore, in terms of
> demand was not of importance a few years ago, but
> it is so now...(South African Digest, 7.12.75)

Even with the efforts of the Government to increase employment in the Reserves and in industries on the borders of the Reserves, the need for African workers in the "white" urban areas increased. Yet these African workers were legally only "visitors," not residents. Much of the housing built in the urban areas was in the form of hostels, which helped the Government prevent African families from living in white areas. Alexandra township, for example, was forcibly changed through the removal of 54,000 residents and the construction of hostels for 30,000 "single" African men and women.

New township suburbs were constructed at Newcastle in Northern Natal in 1974 and 1975 to accommodate employees of the South African Iron and Steel Industrial Corporation's new works. The housing provisions for white employees include 3,195 single family homes, 500 apartments, single quarters for 560 employees, and an apprentice hostel for 300 persons. One hundred and twenty-six apartments were built for Indian employees. A special hostel for 9000 black workers was constructed at Madadeni.

Removals and influx control became even more stringent in the 1970s as African women and children came to be classified as

"superfluous appendages" in the urban areas and were not allowed
to live in the new African towns built in the Reserves near the
border industries unless one parent had a factory job. The effect
of the choice between starving in the Reserves or working under
contract in the urban areas has been for large numbers of mothers
and fathers, married and unmarried, to live in hostels in the
cities, leaving the children in the Reserves for the twelve month
contract period. The sick, the old, the disabled, and the
unemployed lose everything if their lives have been built in the
urban areas, and they are removed.

As was becoming clear in the sixties, the only strength the
African had left was potential withdrawal of labor. Blacks did
not succeed from 1960 on in their opposition to the pass laws,
to removals, to the breaking up of families, to influx controls,
to restrictions on education. But in the area of labor the
Government was forced to recognize the African, and in 1973 passed
legislation granting African workers the right to strike and providing for Works Committees consisting of Africans and employers.
The legislation did not, however, extend the Industrial Conciliation Act provisions to the Reserves. In November 1975 the Government published a bill which provided for establishment of black
industry committees on a regional basis which would have the
authority to negotiate with employers on wages and working
conditions in areas where no Industrial Council agreement exists.

Thus the Government was forced to deal with the reality of
the situation: African workers were organizing and striking, and
white employers were negotiating with them. The employers and the
white unions had come to recognize that unless Africans were
organized into unions officially registered with the Government,
wildcat strikes would increase, employers would have no way of
even knowing when grievances arose, and the entire South African
economy could be jeopardized. Between 1971 and 1973 African
workers in the gold mines achieved a 70 percent increase in pay,
with the men earning in 1973 an average of R43 per month ($60)
plus food and lodging. During the first three months of 1973
nearly 50,000 African workers in Durban closed down 100 companies
by striking for higher wages.

In October 1975 the Prime Minister, B.J. Vorster, addressing
the Steel and Engineering Industries Federation of South Africa
(Seifsa), urged employers in metal and engineering industries
"'to make better use of the available labor from all the population
groups.'" (South African Digest, 31.10.75) The Prime Minister
commended Seifsa for its efforts to train black workers and to
place them in higher skilled jobs.

Also in 1975 the Government opened the first eight industrial
training centers in urban areas for black school children. Three
more were opened in 1976. The training is available to 50,000-
75,000 children, and supplements academic studies. Similar centers
are being opened in the homelands. The South Africa School of
Business Leadership offered a 15-month course for 27 "skilled
Black businessmen" at Hammanskraal, near Pretoria. Only men with
at least three years' experience in business could attend.

During the first seven years of the development of the reserves/

homelands (1963-1970) only 49,000 jobs were developed for Africans, while 900,000 Africans were "repatriated" to the homelands. Yet in the early seventies the Government also began to prohibit black professionals from working not only in white areas but also in the black townships in the urban areas. Black businesses in the townships were also limited to one place of business, or one shop. No more schools were to be allowed except when Africans would set up their own primary schools. All new secondary schools were required to be located in the Reserves. (In 1974 3.6 million black children aged 7-15 attended 11,800 schools having a total of 63,000 teachers – an average of 57 students per teacher and 305 students per school, with an average of 5.3 teachers per school.)

The report by the Xhosa Development Corporation on its first ten years (1965-1975) noted that in the Transkei 12,100 new jobs had been created and Africans now own 474 retail businesses. In Umtata and Butterworth, the two industrial areas in the Transkei, R36,041 million has been committed to industrial projects. But the Transkei still has to import 90 percent of its food.

On May 1, 1975, the Government announced that blacks would be allowed to own homes on a 30-year lease in white areas, a right which had been abolished in 1967. The black, under the new ruling, could also sell the house or leave it to spouse or children, as long as they had legal permission to reside in the white area. In the same announcement the Government granted blacks the right to operate more than one kind of business, to trade in a township and in the homeland area, and to take in a partner. In addition traders and doctors received permission to own premises in black urban residential areas.

In December 1975 the African Bank of South Africa, wholly-owned by blacks, opened in Bophuthatswana, modeled on the Indian-owned Republic Bank in Durban.

In September 1975 the Minister of Defense, P.W. Botha, in statements to the Cape National Party Congress, suggested that South Africans could prevent communism from taking over if they stopped demanding luxuries and worked "for human dignity and better human relations." (South African Digest, 12.9.75.)

In 1972 TUCSA officially changed its policy, again, to endorse full trade union rights for Africans. And in 1973 the Trade Union Congress of Great Britain adopted resolutions to: (1) establish an office in South Africa to organize African trade unions on a large scale, (2) set up an appeal fund for victimized African trade unionists, and (3) urge British companies operating in South Africa to recognize African trade unions.

In 1974, 82 white unions with 366,000 members, 46 Colored or Asian unions with 76,387 members, and 41 mixed unions with 175,543 members were registered. The Trade Union Council had 63 union affiliates with 233,555 members, of whom 28 percent were white and 72 percent Colored or Asian. Nine of the unions were white (30,469 members), 26 Colored or Asian (48,417), and 28 mixed (35,092 white and 119,577 Colored or Asian).

In 1970 the estimated average per capita income for whites was R952; Asians, R147; Coloreds R109; and Africans, R87.

During the seventies the momentum for political opposition

to apartheid shifted to student organizations and to the newly formed Black People's Convention. The Government reacted to them as it had to similar organizations in earlier decades by prohibiting meetings, breaking up demonstrations, and banning and arresting the leaders and participants. None of these organizations, except NUSAS, are multiracial, and the black student and political organizations are separatist in philosophy and action.

The National Party, though threatened by a split from within, continued in the seventies to maintain a large majority in Parliament. The only opposition to Government policy came from the Progressive Party.

On October 10, 1975, the Government celebrated the 100th Anniversary of the formation of Genootskap van Regte Afrikaners (Association of True Afrikaners) by opening the R1 million Pearl of the People monument to the Afrikaans language.

A. Anti-Apartheid Events (1970-1975)

1970   Acquittal of the 20 persons detained with Winnie Mandela and their rearrest.
1970   South African Students Organization (black) and NUSAS demonstrations against arrests, bannings, and removals. (Twenty-five hundred students protested the ban of the 22 defendants in the Winnie Mandela trial in February 1970.)
22.7.1970 Miners' War Dance (150 persons) near Klerksdorp. Threw stones at the police.
7.1972   All-African Women's Conference in Dar-es-Salaam (10th anniversary). (Attended by Albertina Sisulu, Lilian Ngoyi, Helen Joseph, and Mrs. Pillay.)
1972   TUCSA endorsed full trade union rights for Africans.
1973   Black People's Convention (BPC) formed.
1974   Schlebusch Commission investigation of the SAIRR, the Christian Institute, and NUSAS.
1975   SASO/BPC trials.
1975   African appointed Dean of St. George's Cathedral in Johannesburg.

B. The Role of Women in Anti-Apartheid Organizations Trade Unions

In the early seventies women continued to serve as leaders of the industrial trade unions first organized by women in the thirties and forties - clothing and garment workers, liquor and catering workers, tobacco workers, laundry and dry cleaning workers, sweet workers, and food and canning workers. Membership in these unions totaled about 53,000, or 25 percent of all trade union members, and the majority of these unions had white, Colored, and Asian members. Out of 23 unregistered African trade unions in 1973, nine had a woman general secretary. The industries covered by these unions were textile and clothing, tobacco (a separate union for African women), food and canning, laundry and dry-cleaning, and engineering.

In 1974 the following 15 unions, out of a total of 166 registered unions, had a woman general secretary:

	White	Colored/ Asian
Chemical Workers' Union	255	587
East London Liquor and Catering Trades		101
Furniture and Allied Workers Ind. Union (Natal)	9	1,653
Garment Workers' Industrial Union (Natal)	30	25,238
Kimberley Shop Assistants', Warehousemen's and Clerks' Association	361	---
Knitted Fabric Workers' Union	---	128
Laundering, Cleaning, and Dyeing Workers' Union	201	---
National Union of Cigareete and Tobacco Workers	160	380
National Union of Dairy Industry Employees	428	---
National Union of Laundering, Cleaning, and Dyeing Workers	---	1,049
South African Association of Dental Mechanician Employees	33	---
South Africa Theatre Union	433	---
Sweet Workers' Union	110	640
Transvaal Musicians' Union	458	---
Trawler and Line Fishermen's Union	9	710
TOTAL	2,487	30,486

Political Parties. The Progressive Party, the only surviving political party opposed to apartheid, continued to have a woman Member of Parliament in the seventies.

The Black People's Convention, formed as a political organization to achieve black liberation, an egalitarian society, and "an equitable economic system based on the principle and philosophy of black communalism..." (RR 1.73, vol. 35,1), elected a woman as its first president in 1973. She was not re-elected and men took over the leadership of the organization.

Non-white National Organizations. The most active legal non-white, or black, organization in the early seventies was the South African Students Organization (SASO), formed in 1969, which had women members, but not leaders. Then SASO, too, was banned in 1974.

Women continued to be key detainees in Government raids to stop leaflet distribution and underground organizing for the ANC.

Interracial Organizations. The SAIRR along with the Christian Institute and NUSAS became the subject of inquiry for a special Government Commission - the Schlebusch Commission. Nevertheless the SAIRR continued its work with the advice centers - completely organized by women - which tried to get the Government to relieve the arbitrariness of apartheid laws. The SAIRR received a special grant from the Ford Foundation to microfilm and index various archives covering trade unions and political trials. Several women were elected by the membership to serve as representatives on the Executive Committee, and a woman served as President for two years. The SAIRR also adopted a policy position in support of African unions being able to register.

In 1969 the South African Council of Churches and the Christian Institute of Southern Africa initiated the Study Project on Christianity in Apartheid Society (SPRO-CAS). The context for the Project was the "Message to the People of South Africa" issued in September 1968 by the Theological Commission of the South African Council of Churches, which criticized apartheid as "hostile to Christianity." The entire thrust of the Project was toward implementing Christian doctrine. It is not surprising, then, to find (a) very few women participating on the formal Commissions or in the preparation of the reports, and (b) no recognition of the status and problems of women in South Africa.

Staff members of both the Race Relations Institute and the Christian Institute, including several women, were subpoened to testify before the Schlebusch Commission.

The Anglican Church made two major breakthroughs in terms of the status of women in the seventies: several women were ordained and several women became catechists, which allowed them to enter the lower levels of the Church power structure. And a black woman was elected president of the Mothers' Union in the Diocese of Johannesburg.

The Black Sash continued to be involved in programs to alleviate the human suffering caused by apartheid. The Sash maintained and expanded its advice offices in Cape Town, Johannesburg, Durban, and Grahamstown, two being operated in conjuction with the SAIRR, and continued their opposition to the pass laws and influx control. Then in 1971 they issued a nine-point Charter for Women which was presented as a petition to Parliament:

   *Every woman has the right to choose her marriage partner.
   °Every woman has the right to live with her husband throughout
        her married life.
   *Every woman has the right to live with her children, to pro-
        tect them and care for them.
   *Every woman has the right to free education for children.
   *Every woman has the right to own or to rent property in her
        own name.
   *Every woman has the right to freedom of movement and residence.
   *Every woman has the right to work, to free choice of employment,
        and to just and favorable conditions of work.
   *Every woman has the right to live out her declining years with
        those who wish to care for her.
   *Every woman has the right to these fundamental rights and
        freedoms which shall not be violated by any law or
        administrative action.

NUSAS was investigated in 1974 by the Schlebusch Commission, and several of its leaders, including some women, were arrested and banned. NUSAS and the Black Sash held vigils for the release

of the Mandela trial detainees in 1970. In August 357 students
in Johannesburg had their addresses and fingerprints taken by the
police following a demonstration by 600 students. In Durban 1000
students protested the detentions.

During the seventies the National Council of Women (NCW)
took more specific positions on apartheid issues than it had in
earlier decades, and it developed closer liaison with the nationalist women's organizations, including the National Council of
African Women. In the first part of the decade the NCW was particularly involved in the development of home industries in the
resettlement villages in the Reserves. In January 1974 the NCW
wrote the Minister of Labor asking for "'the introduction of a
minimum wage, limited hours of work, payment for overtime, annual
leave, and other conditions applicalbe to labor in industry.'"
(Survey 1974, p. 280) The NCW also urged the Government to amend
the Bantu (Urban Areas) Consolidation Act so that African widows
and divorcees could remain in urban areas.

C. Individual Women in the Anti-Apartheid Movement

As Government control and power increased and the National
Party became the State, information on the anti-apartheid movement
became more and more scarce: the press adopted its own censorship,
laws prevented information being published on prisons or prisoners,
the Government had no obligation to release any information on
detentions or arrests, the courts were subject to the executive
branch...

In the seventies as in the sixties the Government sought to
suppress anti-apartheid political activity. Most of the women who
attempted to be politically active were subjected to bannings and
trials, and even those women active in the more "socially" oriented
organizations, such as the SAIRR, the Christian Institute, NUSAS,
and the Black Sash, came under increasing pressure.

In February 1970 the Attorney General for the Transvaal with-
drew the prosecution against Winnie Mandela and the women and men
charged with her in 1969, but then all were rearrested and detained
under the Terrorism Act.

Rita Alita Ndzanga, one of the 21 accused with Ms. Mandela
in 1969, described in an application to the court beatings and
torture by the police during her imprisonment. She stated that
during the interrogation at the Compol Buildings in Pretoria in
May 1969

> "I fell on the floor. He (the interrogator) then said
> 'staan op' (get up) and attempted to kick me while I
> lay on the floor."

The following morning Ms. Ndzanga made a statement. Then in June
she was asked to make another statement. She refused, and was then
directed to take off her shoes and to stand on three bricks. When
she refused to do this, a member fo the Security Police climbed on
a chair and pulled her by the hair, dropping her on to the bricks.
She fell and hit a gas pipe. This entire process was then repeated.

(Sechaba, May 1970) When she screamed while being treated so
violently, the windows of the interrogation room were closed.

Nomyamise Iris Madikizela also applied to the Supreme Court,
but for the protection of her sister, Nomzamo Winnie Mandela.
She stated that any additional harrassment and suffering might
cause Ms. Mandela to have a physical and mental breakdown. Ms.
Madikizela had herself been held in solitary for six months and
threatened with a ten-year prison term if she did not testify
against her sister.

Finally after having been kept in solitary confinement for
a total of 17 months, the accused were acquitted by the Supreme
Court. They were then placed under bans and house arrests, Ms.
Mandela under 12-hour house arrest, beginning the 30th of September
1970. Upon application Ms. Mandela was allowed to visit her
husband briefly, following which she suffered a mild heart attack.
The police visited the Mandela home frequently, and prosecuted
Iris Madikizela, Mr. Mandela's sister, who had been living in the
home since 1960, for being in Johannesburg illegally and with not
producing a reference book. The magistrate found her guilty but
discharged her because she had not realized she was not on Ms.
Mandela's housing permit.

In the spring of 1973 Zinzie Mandela, 12 year old daughter
of Winnie and Nelson Mandela, wrote the United Nations Committee
on Apartheid expressing her fear that "'something terrible is
going to happen to mummy.'" Her mother, banned and under house
arrest in Johannesburg, had recently been the victim of a series
of attacks and robberies, including one attack on her life.
(Sechaba, May 1973)

Joyce Sikakane, banned along with the other defendants in the
Winnie Mandela trial, was reported in 1974 to have disappeared from
her parents' home in Orlando West, Soweto, near Johannesburg.
Ms. Sikakane had spent most of her childhood in the home of her
grandfather, the late Revd. A.M. Sikakane, a founder of the
African National Congress. There she came to know as a child
Chief Luthuli and other ANC leaders and defendants in the 1956
Treason Trials. She had been sent to her grandfather's because
of the closing of the schools in 1954 by the Anglican Church upon
passage of the Bantu Education Act. E. Modisane reports Ms.
Sikakane's account of the arrest of her grandfather for the Treason
Trials:

'The police, she said, arrived at my grandfather's
house armed with what I later learned were sten guns.
I was very shocked for this was the first time I saw
a gun. This struck me as absurd and I realized that
something was very wrong. My grandfather was such a
peaceful man. I had never seen him quarrel with anyone or utter a harsh word in all the years I stayed
with him. Yet, the police had taken him away after
raiding our house for several hours, as if he was a
common criminal.' (Sechaba, January 1974)

Following completion of her degree in political science at

the University of South Africa Joyce Sikakane had found a job as a
reporter for The World, a paper catering to African readers but
owned by whites, and emphasizing stories on crime, sex, and social-
ites, not on politics and the concerns and living conditions of
blacks in South Africa. At the time of her arrest she was working
as a reporter for the Rand Daily Mail, covering stories of mass
removals and their effects on families.

Shanthie Naidoo, who had been under a banning order since 1963,
and had been imprisoned in 1969 and kept in solitary confinement
for 369 days for refusing to testify against Ms. Mandela, in 1971
applied for a permanent exit permit. The permit was granted, but
her application to be allowed to go to a point of departure was
denied. Ms. Naidoo, along with Winnie Mandela, Violet Weinberg,
and Ilse Fischer (daughter of Bram Fischer) were detained again
in 1971. Finally in September 1972 Shantie Naidoo was granted
permission to leave South Africa, on the condition that she
refrain from political activities. She left in October.

Martha Dlamini was held in jail under the Terrorism Act for
over a year in 1970 following the acquittal of the 22 in the
Winnie Mandela trial. (Her husband was then president of SACTU.)
Gladys Manzi (African) was banned and restricted. Vivi Gulsrud,
a Norwegian journalist, was arrested for being in an African
township without a permit. Winifred Khalipha and Mabel Mali were
sentenced to eight years in prison for ANC and terrorist activities.

Eve Behrman was one of four whites detained in Johannesburg
in November 1971. They were released on bail, and after three
postponements of hearings, left the country illegally.

Among numbers of men and women detained in 1971 were Fatima
Essop and her brother, Mahommed, a medical student in Johannesburg.
Mr. Essop was found by his father in serious physical condition in
a hospital a few days after he was detained. A month later another
sister was also detained.

In October 1971 Amina Desai was the only woman among four
Indians arrested and held in solitary until charged and convicted
in 1972 under the Terrorism Act with preparing to distribute
leaflets by bucket bombs and with furthering the aims of the ANC
and the SACP. She was sentenced to six years in prison and was
refused leave to appeal. Ms. Desai was accused by the Government
of having allowed Mr. Timol (see below) to use her home to decode
secret letters, prepare to mail ANC leaflets, and experiment with
gunpowder. Ms. Desai, a widow living alone, testified Mr. Timol
was like one of the family and had free access to her home.

During the 1972 trial of Mr. Essop testimony was introduced
stating that Ahmed Timol (who had died during detention in 1971)
had received guerilla and subversive training at the home of Rica
and Jack Hodgson in London and theoretical training in communist
doctrines from Stephanie Kemp, also then living in London. Messrs.
Timol and Essop were to have had coded messages from "Stephanie,"
ANC leaflets, and SACP publications in their possession when they
were arrested.

The Government actions to prohibit anti-apartheid activities
continued to affect women involved in a variety of activities and
situations.

Allison Norman was identified by the prosecution in the trial of the Anglican Dean of Johannesburg, G.A. ffrench-Beytagh, as being the person who sent R51,400 to the Dean from Defense and Aid for assistance to political prisoners and their families. Ms. Norman lived in England and refused to go to South Africa to testify without a guarantee that no proceedings would be initiated against her. The guarantee was not given.

Then in 1973 banning orders were renewed for a third term of five years on Mary Moodley of Benoni and Jacqueline Arenstein of Durban, and in 1974 on Albertina Sisulu. The banning order on Amina Cachalia was relaxed. Ms. R. Becher, a pastor of the Methodist Church who worked with the Colored community in Cape Town from 1967 on, had her application for residence permit renewal denied.

In 1971, after eight and a half years, Helen Joseph's house arrest was lifted when she was in the hospital for a major cancer operation. At the end of October 1972 when her and Molly Anderson's banning orders expired, they were not renewed, but the women remained "listed." (In November 1973 Helen Joseph was one of fifty Black Sash demonstrators protesting the banning under the SCA of 70 people.)

In June 1975 Jennifer Roxburgh, a lecturer in African studies, was one of three members of the law faculty of Natal University arrested under the Terrorism Act; and in September Megan Riley was one of five people associated with NUSAS arrested at the University of Cape Town, under the same Act, and detained without trial, in connection with the visit and arrest of Breyten Breytenback, the exiled Afrikaans poet and critic of apartheid.

In 1972 the Black People's Convention (BPC) was formed with Winnifred Kgware elected president by the 200 African, Colored, and Asian delegates at the first national congress. Although Ms. Kgware was the only BPC leader not banned in 1973, she was not elected to a leadership position in 1974.

Daphne Masekele spoke at the convention stressing the need for blacks to function as blacks, not as people seeking to gain what whites have. The preamble for the BPC adopted at the convention stated "... Black political movements are the only media through which our liberation and emancipation can be effected and realized." (Sechaba, October 1972) Lindelwa Mabandla, a shool teacher, was among the members of BPC banned in 1974.

On August 30, 1973, Sumboornam Pillay Moodley, a 25-year old Indian research assistant with Black Community Programmes (BCP) and assistant publications director of the South African Students' Organization, received a five-year banning order and 12-hour house arrest. (Her mother had been active in the SAIC in the fifties.) Ms. Moodley had obtained an arts degree in speech and drama at the University of Durban, but was terminated as a high school teacher by the Department of Indian Affairs in 1972. She was also a founder of the Theatre Council of Natal (Tecon) which presented anti-apartheid plays.

When the officers of SASO were banned and arrested in 1973 and 1974, Ms. Soma Reddi, previously senior assistant at the SASO head office in Durban, took over national leadership along with Ben Langa.

Then she, too, was banned. Also among the SASO members banned in 1974 was Dr. Vuyi Mashabalala, wife of the banned secretary-general of the now defunct University Christian Movement.

NUSAS leaders also experienced a series of bannings and arrests in 1973. The Schlebusch Commission had investigated NUSAS as well as the SAIRR and the Christian Institute following the massive student demonstrations protesting detention without trial, banning of student leaders and teachers, and restrictions on student organizations. Following the interim report of the Schlebusch Commission eight NUSAS leaders were banned, including two women, Paula Ensor (one of two vice presidents and secretary-general of NUSWEL-Welfare) and Sheila Lapinsky (permanent general-secretary). All eight were prohibited from entering educational institutions.

In 1972 a number of NUSAS members had been arrested during the organization's Free Education campaign. One of the 14 persons convicted under the Riotous Assemblies Act in connection with the campaign was Dr. Helen King, wife of the Anglican Dean of Cape Town. Dr. King was convicted of assaulting a police officer, but was discharged.

In 1971 the Natal Indian Congress was revived by Ela and Mewa Ramgobin. When Mewa Ramgobin was banned in 1972, Ela (a grand-daughter of Mahatma Gandhi) took his place as head of the Congress. Nokukhanya Luthuli, wife of Albert Luthuli, opened the first convention of the revived NIC in 1972.

Ms. Ramgobin also ran her husband's insurance brokerage office in Durban following his banning and house arrest. Then she, too, received banning orders and was placed under house arrest - on August 31, 1973. A social worker, Ms. Ramgobin was restricted to the Inanda district, and forbidden to take part in BCP or SASO activities.

In the report of the Schlebusch Commission's inquiries into the SAIRR, published in 1974, the Institute's youth program came under particular attack. Following release of the report the African organizers were detained, including Brigitte Mabandla (September 1974). After six months in detention Ms. Mabandla was released, no charge having been brought against her, and she returned in April to the SAIRR staff as Youth Programme Organizer in Natal. In her position with the SAIRR, Ms. Mabandla organized and operated the SAIRR Winter School for black children. Then late in 1975 she and her husband were banished to a rural area.

Two other women were sentenced to fine or jail in connection with the Schlebusch Commission's inquiries: Dorothy Cleminshaw, who worked in the SPRO-CAS Cape Town office, and Ilona Kleinschmidt, an assistant organizer for SPRO-CAS. Both had refused to testify before the Commission. Other staff members called to testify included Justine Pike (SAIRR secretary), Muriel Horrell (SAIRR Research Officer), and Joyce Bentley-Smith (SAIRR Finance Officer).

The July 26, 1974, Government Gazette, listed the following women as banned under the Suppression of Communism Act (out of a total of 185 people):

Jacqueline Arenstein
Mabel Balfour
Amina Cachalia
Jeanette Marguerite Cunningham-Brown
Martha Litha Dhlamini
Margaret Paula Ensor
Gertrude Gelb
Sheila Barsel Lapinsky
Lindelwas Mtutuzeli Mabandla
Nomzamo Winnie Mandela
Tshintsheng Caroline Mashaba
Virginia (Venus) Mngoma
Mary Moodley
Sumboornam Pillay Moodley
Indris Elathenator Naidoo
Phyllis Ruth Vasendha Naidoo
Rita Alita Ndzanga
Soma Lynette Reddi
Leslie Erica Schermbrucker
Joyce Sikakane
Albertina Sisulu
Elizabeth van der Heyden
Violet May Weinberg
Gwendoline Edith Wilcox

Women who had for years been active in the SAIRR achieved
recognition in the seventies: in 1970 Dr. Ellen Hellman received
the medal of the Royal African Society for dedicated service to
Africa; Dr. Sheila van der Horst served as President of the
Institute from 1970-1971; both she and Dr. Hansi Pollak were
elected Honorary Life Members of the SAIRR. Dr. Hellman stated
the Royal African Society award was "an encouragement to all who,
like the Institute, are committed to seek racial conciliation by
peaceful means, to lessen inequality, and to advance along the
hard road to greater social justice." (RR News, November 1970)
In January of 1973 Dr. Hellman urged that every effort be made to
get blacks into the trade union movement, to get black unions
registered. (RR News, February 1973) Dr. van der Horst continued
to serve as a member of the Cape Western Regional Committee and of
the Research Committee, the latter being chaired by Dr. Hellman.
Van der Horst is Associate Professor of Economics at the University
of Cape Town and has published several articles and books on
African workers, distribution of income, industrial relations, and
race relations.
    Dr. Pollak had served as Chairman of the SAIRR Natal Region
from 1954-1960 and of the Cape Region from 1969-1973. She was a
member of the Executive Committee from 1954 on, being elected Vice
President several times. Dr. Pollak is Professor of Sociology and
Social Work at Cape Town University and was responsible for
organizing several studies and seminars on Black Consciousness and
on general racial matters. In 1971 the Progressive Party appointed
Dr. Pollak to head their standing committee on The Family.
    Several other women served in leadership roles in the regional

sections of the SAIRR, including Dr. Sylvia Kaplan, Vice-Chairman of the Natal Region; Mrs. I. Perlman, secretary of the Southern Transvaal Region; and Jo Thorpe, regional secretary in Natal. Ann Perry has been the Research Officer in the Durban office for years, in which capacity she conducted a study of employment of educated Africans. Ms. Perry was also a member of the multi-racial International Women's Year Natal Committee. Muriel Horrell has continued publication of the annual Survey and of other research reports. Nancy Charton prepared a study on "The Unemployed African in Grahamstown," finding that 24 percent of the men over 18 were unemployed, and she participated in the Abe Bailey Institute of Inter-Racial Studies' "A Study of White South African Elites."

Mrs. P. Ramasar and Ann Perry presented two of the four papers at a 1972 SAIRR symposium on "Conditions and Problems in African, Colored, and Indian Residential Areas in South Africa's Cities." In 1973 the Natal Region of the SAIRR held a multi-racial workshop on "Women in Society: A Challenge to Change" at which Ann Perry, Dora Mabiletsa, Margaret Rajbally, and Rosemary Starkey spoke on "Cultural Stereotypes"; Luli Webster on "Women in Education"; Margaret Bolton on "Women as Workers"; and Zubi Seedat on "Women's Legal Status."

During the seventies several projects involving domestic workers emerged. The initiative came from Audrey Cobden, whose ideas were implemented in Sue Gordon's SAIRR/Wilgespruit Fellowship Centre Domestic Workers' and Employers' Project (DWEP). In 1973 Ms. Gordon published the 70 page booklet "Domestic Workers: A Handbook for Housewives" in which she recommended a minimum cash wage for domestic worker who lives in, for a 5 1/2 day work week of 8 hours a day, of R45 per month; a minimum daily rate of R3 for 8 hours, plus transportation expenses and lunch, for a daily worker; and a minimum hourly rate of 60 cents. In the booklet Ms. Gordon also recommends the employer provide satisfactory accommodations, including a shower or bath; hot and cold running water; heat; provision for warming food; medical care; holidays; and old age pension.

Through DWEP by 1974 seventeen "Centres of Concern" had been established on the Witwatersrand by groups of white housewives and churchwomen living in the area, with the intent that the domestic workers would take over operation of the Centres. Additional Centres have been established in Cape Town, Port Elizabeth, Pietermaritzburg, East London, Durban, and Pretoria. By August 1975 some twenty Centres of Concern for domestic workers were operating in Pietermaritzburg and Durban alone. The Centres provide classes in reading and writing, dressmaking, cooking, typing, first-aid, home-nursing, and driving.

Qedusizi Buthelezi, who obtained her Bachelor of Arts degree at the University of Ngoye in KwaZulu, joined DWEP early in 1975 as an assistant organizer whose main concern is to raise the self-image and self-esteem of domestic workers. In this process she helps the workers to form committees and to run Centres of Concern. Audrey Cobden, the iniator of DWEP, became the Natal full-time organizer in 1975. (Mrs. Cobden had served as secretary of the Southern Transvaal Region of the Institute in 1970-1971.) In 1975 she organized a rally of domestic workers held in the Durban City Hall.

In 1974 Maphiri Masekela and Pusetso Letlabika set up a domestic workers project for the South Africa Council of Churches. Maggie Oewies and Myrtle Michaels, Colored domestic workers, began in 1973 with the Young Christian Workers to organize groups of domestic workers to discuss problems faced by young women moving into an urban area. They also published a pamphlet, "But Madam," for the workers.

In 1973 Mrs. Mahlasela, wife of the Methodist minister in New Brighton, established a literacy training program in the township. The Catholic Church, by 1975, was running a Bureau of Literacy and Literature with seven full-time instructors, five men and two women. One of the women, Sheila Frew, organized two courses in 1975 to train a total of 21 teachers at Centres of Concern in East London. The second women, Melmoth Podi, offered courses in Mabopane township near Pretoria. By July 1975, 16,000 mineworkers had completed literacy courses. The Women's Association of African Independent Churches also began providing literacy courses in the seventies, for which Lindy Myeza is a key organizer.

In 1971 Jean Sinclair, national president of the Black Sash, released the nine-point Charter for Women, which later was introduced as a petition in Parliament in February 1971 by Helen Suzman. In 1972 Ms. Sinclair, after participating in a project to find out what happens to a person living on the average African old age pension of R5 per month, wrote the Minister of Bantu Development that she had experienced lethargy, tiredness, irritability, depression, and feeling cold. Ms. Sinclair and the new Black Sash president in 1975, Sheena Duncan, led the Black Sash in speaking out against migrant labor, which produced broken homes; poverty; starvation; malnutrition; and low wages. The organization concentrated in the early seventies on fighting apartheid, exposing injustice, and trying to establish meaningful contact across color lines. Members consistently demonstrated against the lack of representation in Parliament of 80 percent of the South African people, detention without charge or trial, bannings, police violence, removals, and living conditions in the hostels. In July 1975 Ms. Duncan led the opposition to the Government's proposed "rehabilitation institutions" in the Reserves, likening them to Soviet or Nazi prison camps. (NYT 20.7.75)

Ms. R.H. Robb continued in the seventies as director of the Athlone Advice Center, operated by the Black Sash, which handles several thousand complaints per year. Black Sash members prepared several talks and publications on the effects of apartheid, including "The Plight of the Urban African," by Sheena Duncan; "Who Cares?" a pamphlet on the effect of apartheid and removals on African women; and an article on inter-racial contact still permissible by law. Jean Chase of the Black Sash wrote a description of her experiment in breaking down petty apartheid through treating her maid as an equal on a shopping tour.

Sheena Duncan also chaired the Johannesburg Anglican Diocesan Challenge group, the diocesan program for human relations. She made the following comment on her experience as a delegate to the

1975 Anglican Provincial Synod:

> 'It enabled me to see what it is to be on the
> receiving end of paternalism. Everyone was
> exceedingly considerate and ever so humorously
> tolerant. They kept telling me how lucky I
> was to be there - as if it was the Rand Club -
> and endlessly quoted St. Paul about women
> being silent in the councils of the church.'
> (<u>Seek</u> 5.75)

The only free and voluntary legal advice center, besides the
Black Sash/SAIRR centers, available to people of all races during
the first half of the seventies, was located in Johannesburg and
directed by Pauline Lipson. Attorneys associated with the center
provide legal services without charge. In 1971 the center handled
an average of 1,072 civil and criminal cases per month. Felicia
Kentridge actively worked with the SAIRR to expand such legal
services.

SPRO-CAS involved very few women in its official commissions.
Nancy Charton was the only woman among the 21 members of the
Political Commission; Fatima Meer and Mrs. R. Selsick worked with
the Social Commission (the only women out of a total of 19 people)
while Ann Hope (training and education consultant) was the only
woman, out of 14 people, to sign the report; Dr. Sheila van der
Horst was the only woman on the Economic Commission; Anne Adams
and Mrs. J. Raikes were the only women out of six people assisting
the Education Commission, and no women were members of or consul-
tants to that Commission.

Barbara M. Grieve, president of the National Council of Women
of South Africa, participated in 1972 in the petition to the Government protesting police action against students and urging free and
equal education for all races. She stated in letters to the Government and to the press: "Women's struggle against discrimination
has been maintained for decades. We have suffered from that based
on sex. We uphold those who now oppose discrimination based on
race." (<u>NCW News</u>, vol. 38, no. 1, July 1972) In 1974 Ms. Grieve
emphasized in her address at the fortieth annual congress of the
NCW "that because normal freedom of association was difficult in
South Africa, a real effort must be made to achieve mutual under-
standing with members of black groups." (<u>RR Survey</u> 1974, p. 51)

Monica Wilson, for years active in the <u>SAIRR</u>, gave the
Bertha Solomon Memorial Lecture for the NCW in 1974, in which she
dealt with the problems created by the migrant labor system for
urban and rural African women. She urged that African widows and
divorcees be allowed to remain in urban areas in their own right.

In 1971 NUSAS elected Helen Joseph honorary president for
1972. Although Ms. Joseph's banning order had been suspended, she
was still "listed" and so could not become a member of any organization which was critical of Government policy, and so had to
decline the invitation. NUSAS then decided to leave the office
vacant for the year.

In 1972 Mrs. R.J. Small was one of four faculty members at

the University of the Western Cape who opposed efforts by the Government and university officials to prohibit student organizing by the South African Students' Organization.

The University Christian Movement, organized in the late sixties as a multi-racial organization, elected Isabel Direko as national president in 1971. The UCM became defunct in 1972 under pressures relating to its existence as a multi-racial organization of students.

The two members of Parliament in the seventies who most actively opposed legislation relating to apartheid and police powers were Catherine D. Taylor, MP for Wynberg in the Cape, a member of the United Party, and Helen Suzman, MP for Johannesburg, and member of the Progressive Party.

Ms. Taylor took particular interest in legislation affecting education and affecting Colored people. In 1970 she stated in the Assembly the Colored people were "sick of being treated as second-class citizens in their own country," (RR Survey 1970, p. 12; Hansard 11 cols. 5212 et seg.) and she described the problems created for the Colored people by the Government's ideologies, especially the declaration of District Six in Cape Town as a white area. In 1971 Ms. Taylor opposed the Extention of the University Education Act which regulated non-white student registration. She wanted the universities to have the authority to decide on admission of non-whites. She also raised in Parliament the problem of the tremendous shortage of schools for African children living in urban areas - one secondary school for every 80,000 Africans.

In 1972 she made a motion in Parliament to prevent passage of the Colored Persons' Representative Council Amendment Act on the grounds it would take power away from the Council and would not deal with the real problem - that the Government had not given the Colored people a fully elected Council. (The Labor Party had won the elections and the Government through appointments had given control of the Council to the pro-Government/pro-apartheid Federal Party.)

In 1970 Ms. Taylor accused Sgt. Andries van Wyke, on the floor of Parliament, of assaulting Imam Abdullah Haron while he was in the custody of the Security Police and of causing the decline in health which ended in the Imam's death.

Ms. Taylor spoke out in 1973 against the United Party participation in the Schlebusch Commission, and their not producing a minority report once they did participate. She noted that even though she specialized in educational matters and the affairs of Colored people, she was not appointed as a United Party representative on the Schlebusch Commission or on the Commission of Inquiry into Matters Relating to the Colored Population, chaired by Erika Theron, professor at the University of Stellenbosch.

The United Party told Ms. Taylor several times not to criticize UP policy and action, and in 1973 threatened to expel her from the Party caucus. She then resigned as UP shadow Minister of Education, and announced she would not seek reelection.

Helen Suzman continued in the 1970s to raise questions on police activity, prison conditions, people detained and banned, and crime statistics. She opposed every piece of oppressive legislation and took steps to maximize the recognition of the Reserves and the role of their leaders in determining South African policy and affairs. Ms. Suzman urged recognition of African trade unions, or, at a minimum, formation of the legal Works Committees, and repeal of the Immorality Act.

Another woman from the United Party, Anna Scheepers, for years president of the Garment Workers Union, entered Parliament as a Senator in 1974, speaking in favor of recognition of African unions. In the Senate she pointed out the effect on union costs of the Government requiring "mixed" unions to separate activities by race, and she urged the Government to hold hearings on the desirability of amending the Industrial Conciliation Act to include Africans as "employees."

For nearly four decades Ms. Scheepers and Johanna Cornelius, both of the GWU, had urged the Government to recognize African unions. They pointed out that wildcat strikes, riots, and work stoppages were inevitable if the majority of workers (the Africans) had no legal means to organize and negotiate. They also opposed attempts by the Government in 1972 to allow unions in the Homelands to be controlled by the Homeland governments.

In 1971 Ms. Scheepers had urged that industries be established closer to urban non-white townships so that the absenteeism of non-white workers might be reduced and productivity improved. And in 1973 she was the only woman out of 12 speakers invited to present papers at the Abe Bailey Institute of Inter-Racial Studies and the Trade Union Council of South Africa workshop on "The Responsibility of Organized Labor in a Developing Plural Society."

In 1973 Ms. Scheepers was elected vice-president of TUCSA and chair of the Transvaal Clothing Industry Medical Benefit Society. That year marked her 34th anniversary as president of the Garment Workers' Union of South Africa.

In 1975 the President of South Africa appointed Alathea A. Jansen Chairman of the executive of the Colored Persons Representative Council. Ms. Jansen was appointed to the CRC in March as an Independent. She was also the first recipient of the Elsie Simmern Memorial Award presented by the Association of Country Women of the World, and she represented South Africa at the 1974 United Nations World Population Congress.

Stella Sigcau (African) was the first South African woman to attain cabinet rank: in 1969 she was appointed Minister of Roads and Public Works, and in 1975, Minister of the Interior, in the Transkei government. She is also honorary life president of the South Africa Federation of Business and Professional Women.

Lucy Mvubelo, general secretary of the National Union of Clothing Workers since 1968, visited the United States in 1971 and urged American businesses to promote change within South Africa by increasing the wages of non-white employees, providing new benefits, and training non-whites for higher skilled positions. Ms. Mvubelo opposed the view that the "Works Committees" legislated by the Government provided representation of African workers. (The SAIRR found in a 1974 survey only 28 such committees even existed.) Ms. Mvubelo urged extension of union rights to African workers, but despite this position was refused the opportunity to speak at the

July 1974 Geneva Conference of the International Labor Organization, because of her "cooperation" with the South African Government. In an interview with the Race Relations News (published November 1974) Lucy Mvubelo stated the black states believe "that I as a Black trade unionist may have been briefed by the Government to attend the conference. Or that I am an agent of the Government..." She urged that the laws be changed rapidly to allow Africans full rights through peaceful means.

Harriet Bolton, secretary of the 20,000 member black (mainly Indian and Colored) Garment Workers' Industrial Union in Natal, represented TUCSA at the International Labor Organization's June 1973 session. In 1974 she became active in organizing other black unions. When her three key organizers (all men) were banned in 1974, she and the Natal union threatened to withdraw from TUCSA because TUCSA had refused to oppose the banning. Ms. Bolton accused TUCSA leaders of trying to prevent union officials from being politically active. She stated that TUCSA resolutions to organize black workers

'are little more than pious lip-service. They are primarily designed to white-wash South Africa in the eyes of the world trade union movement, the ILO, the British TUC and foreign visitors and diplomats.' (Sechaba, May 1974, p. 7)

During the seventies women served as the general secretary of nine out of 23 unregistered African trade unions:

Lucy Mvubelo	National Union of Clothing Workers
I. Dlamini	General Factory Workers' Benefit Fund
G. Biyela	National Union of Textile Workers
Jane Hlongwane	Engineering and Allied Workers' Union
J. Gumede	Union of Clothing and Allied Workers
E. Seloro	Textile Workers' Union (Transvaal)
A. Molefe	Laundry and Dry Cleaning Workers
C. du Preez	Tobacco Workers' Union of African Women
L. Sibona	African Food and Canning Union

The largest black union is the National Union of Clothing Workers, 22 years old in 1975, with a membership of 18,000 workers. The second largest black union, the Engineering and Allied Workers' Union, with 7,000 members, was 14 years old in 1975. The secretary of the latter union, Jane Hlongwane, summed up the status of black unions in an interview with the New York Times: "'We have to educate people not to fear the white man. Most workers feel that management is all-powerful. If you tell them their numbers make them powerful as well, they still can't appreciate this until they see it in action...The manager feels he understands the black man without really doing so...When a strike comes, he thinks there's a Communist in the factory.'" (June 10, 1975)

Other women trade union leaders in the seventies included Mrs. M. Young, secretary of the 1,000 member Witwatersrand Tea Room, Restaurant and Catering Trade Employees' Union; Mrs. N.G. Forsyth, general secretary of the 875 member European Liquor and Catering Trades Employees Union; Liz Abrahams, general secretary of the 8,837 member Food and Canning Workers' Union; and Johanna Cornelius, secretary of the 11,000 member Garment Workers' Union of South Africa and general secretary of the 42,321 member Garment Workers' Unions' Consultative Committee, of which Anna Scheepers is the chair.

Johanna Cornelius participated on a SAIRR panel on "Labor Relations and the Future of Trade Unionism" in January 1973 at which she stated that the ICA as amended in 1956 had caused the deterioration of the trade union movement in South Africa. She urged that the Wage Act be scrapped and the ICA amended to include African workers in the definition of "employee." Through these steps all workers would be subject to the same legislation in the same way.

Women served in several social welfare posts, through which they ameliorated some of the effects of apartheid, or themselves broke apartheid barriers. Four women - Anna Watkins, J. Oberholzer, S.E. van Niekerk, and E.M. Dowling - were members of the ten member multi-racial delegation from South Africa to the International Union for Child Welfare Conference in Kenya in 1975. Dr. Margaret Barker spent 30 years in KwaZulu practicing pediatrics. Dr. K.N. Ginwala (Indian woman) is deputy medical superintendent at the H.H. Khan Provincial Hospital in Durban and is advisor on health matters to the National Council of Women. Ms. Jean Labuschagne developed programs to help working African women in conjunction with the Katatura Ladies Club in Windhoek, South West Africa.

Constance Ntshona spoke at a University of Witwatersrand Focus on Women course during which she pointed out

'And your children...some of you have children who were born in Johannesburg. If you were Black you would not be permitted to bring these children to live with you. A child born in Kyalami would not be permitted to live with you in Houghton.

If you were living in Parktown North now and the Government declared that all family accommodation in that suburb had to be destroyed and that hostels for single people must be built instead, you might be ordered to live in a female hostel. Your husband could be ordered to live in a men's hostel. Your children would be sent to the homelands.

These things are happening every day to families in Alexandra.' (RR News, March 1975)

The visible anti-apartheid movement in the seventies continued to include a large number of women, again dealing with survival issues and problems of daily life. The organizations, except those having all women members, still tended to have male officials and women workers. What was happening in the underground opposition, sabotage, and guerilla efforts is impossible to ascertain. Many women who had been active in the anti-apartheid movement in earlier decades and had escaped or left South Africa on exit permits continued to be active in exile, but none were officers of the ANC or the PAC.

A few women officially represent anti-apartheid organizations: Kate Molale is the ANC representative on the Women's International Democratic Federation Secretariat; Zola Zembe was SACTU's representative at the Anti-Apartheid Movement's Trade Union Conference in 1973 (England); Ruth Mompati served on the ANC delegation to the First World Congress of Peace Forces, held in Moscow in 1973; Magdalene Resha is an ANC representative with the Pan African Women's Congress.

The seventies find South African women in much the same position as the twenties. Both the African and the white power structures - political, economic, religious, and social - are male-dominated, but the major changes taking place are the result of the concerted pressures and organizing of and by women.

CHAPTER 9

IX.   CONCLUSION

The policy of apartheid continues to govern South Africa
today. But a few aspects have been relaxed: the removals to the
Reserves have slowed down, the "whites only" and "non-whites only"
signs are being removed, black professionals and businesses are
being allowed to operate in urban areas, integrated teams and
delegations are representing South Africa at international events
and conferences.

The anti-apartheid movement in the seventies is multi-faceted,
running the full gamut from armed guerillas and saboteurs to the
domestic workers' Centres of Concern. The movement is much
broader than in the early decades of the century, and includes a
much larger number of people. In the twenties the people opposed
to discrimination were involved in trade union organizing, setting
up multi-racial organizations, political campaigns, meetings with
Government officials and representatives, and opposition to the
pass laws and to poor working conditions. In the seventies people
actively opposed to apartheid still include those involved in trade
union organizing of black workers, in black political development,
in literacy projects, and in continuing multi-racial organizations
and events. But a thrust toward undermining the Government and
the economy by use of violence has replaced the political activity
of the twenties and the meetings with public officials, and social
welfare programs operated by non-Government organizations have
replaced the Government's social programs of the twenties.

The continuing Government policy of apartheid has created
severe human suffering in South Africa. To try to alleviate that
human suffering has become a political, and an anti-apartheid,
activity. Evidence of human concern was not so construed in the
twenties.

The impact of the anti-apartheid movement during the past 50
years has been both positive and negative from the perspective of
the goal of achieving equal opportunity for people of all races:

Positive:
   Multi-racial trade unions
   Increase in wages of black and women workers and improvements
      in working conditions
   Self-awareness of black students and leaders
   Alleviation of some social and economic deprivations through
      protests and political pressures
   Independence of the Transkei (though also negative), one of
      the "tribal homelands" set aside for Africans
   Financial assistance to the Reserves/Homelands for agricultural
      and industrial development
   Relaxation of "petty" apartheid

Negative:
      Role of other nations in providing financial support for the
            opposition (dependency created)
      Increase in police and defense spending and power
      Repression and violence resulting from protests, sabotage,
            and guerilla activities
      Informants system
      Implementation of apartheid policy through actual formation
            of tribal states/nations, forced removals, and hostel
            living

      The above is not to say that the present police state powers
of the Government are the result of anti-apartheid activities alone.
Clearly the insecurity and elitist attitudes of an Afrikaner
closed society had within itself the seeds for a police state.
The anti-apartheid violence and resulting fear, though, helped set
the tone for acceptance of "order" over "freedom."
      The anti-apartheid movement did force the whites of South
Africa to decide whether or not discrimination is official policy.
The policy of separateness, "apartheid," cannot be implemented in
a country whose economy and social life depends on cheap black
labor. The compromises within apartheid ideology necessary to
maintain the white way of life mean increased hardship for blacks
and increased polarization between blacks and whites. Normal life
for black families, as known by American families, is becoming
less and less possible.
      This polarization and tension is to some extent a result of
the nati-apartheid efforts, and may well end in revolution -
violent or not. If a revolution occurs, though, it will not come
from the existing anti-apartheid organizations. It will be an
uprising caused by unbearable tension and suffering or a collapse
caused by the sheer weight of inhuman demands and restrictions.
Either way the rigid Government system will fall and chaos will
ensue.
      Where are the women in all this? Consistently throughout
the last five decades it has been the women who were least willing
to tolerate the oppression, least able to adapt. This is most
likely the result of their not receiving even any token of recognition. The men's labor is valued and recognized as essential.
And the men would give up all for the jobs, for the city life, for
the tiny piece of power, of place in the existing structure. Many
black men were able to become ministers, doctors, and lawyers,
leaders in national and multi-racial organizations. Women had no
such potential except in the fifties and in the trade unions.
      The impact of the women's activities within the anti-apartheid
movement has a different tone from the overall movement impact.
Over the years the women

Organized multi-racial unions and negotiated industrial conciliation
      agreements for workers of all races
Improved the working conditions and wages of women factory workers
      of all races
Maintained the only consistent anti-apartheid voice in Parliament

100

Organized the large anti-pass demonstrations and the Congress of
    the People (1955)
Prevented the pass from being extended to women until 1960
Eased the impact of apartheid on people's daily lives
Conducted research and public education campaigns revealing the
    actual effects of Government policy and activity on people
Opposed and counteracted Government education practices and
    Christian National Education
Maintained the pressure for recognition of African trade unions
    and development of a trade union movement
Developed close ties among women of different races

The women in the anti-apartheid movement seem to be much
closer than the men. Women of all races stood together in the
face of Government oppression, and worked together in common
activities. The women organized separately from the men. Generally
the men, black and white, excluded women from their associations.
Perhaps because of this when the women did act, they joined together in common cause to oppose a common enemy. This identity
against an enemy simply was not possible for men, except for the
communists who ideologically opposed the power structure and the
economic system, and the blacks who ideologically opposed whites.
The exception to this pattern of cooperation among women of
all races is the Black Sash which for seven years excluded all but
white women. And these women came from the upper middle class,
having experienced all the benefits of wealth and comfort gained
at the expense of people of another race.
The women overall have not used violence as a tactic, and men
have excluded women from their sabotage and guerilla activities
except for supportive roles. To take up a gun against a social,
economic, political, and religious system seems awkward, at best,
to most women. The gun is a male perception of solving problems.
And the men know this. The decision to turn to violence could
almost be read as an escape into what is most familiar to men:
talk or guns. If talk doesn't work, the alternative is violence.
The women had begun to organize the people and the workers.
But organizing is long hard work, with few measurable results.
The male Government cannot deal with this approach either. They
haven't yet figured out how to stop the organizing of workers,
the organizing of domestics, the literacy programs, or even the
public meetings and protests organized by the women.
If the anti-apartheid movement can be viewed as successful in
some area, the long range impact, except for the effects of the
acts of violence and of the individual male leaders - who are
perceived as heroes and role-models more than a woman could ever
be - , is directly related to efforts of the women in trade union
organizing, in public education, and in public demonstrations and
protests. The violence is not to be discounted, however, for it
does produce the conscious recognition of the confrontation which
people are feeling in their desperate and depressing efforts to
survive. And the male heroes in prison and in exile also play an
important role in identifying the cause and the goal for the future.
The women, though, remain the guts of the on-going resistance to

apartheid. But they will never gain the opportunity to reconstruct society even if a revolution does occur. The men, black and white, control the economic and military power, and they all exclude women. Until women become equals with men in both the black and white organizations, and until economic, social, religious, and political systems open up to all people, no just society will be possible in South Africa.

CHAPTER 10

X. APPENDICES

APPENDIX A. SUPPRESSION OF COMMUNISM ACT, 1950

In terms of the Suppression of Communism Act, 1950, as amended by legislation of 1951, 1962, 1963, 1964, 1965, 1966, 1967, 1968, and 1972, "communism" means the doctrine of Marxian socialism or any related form of that doctrine, and includes any doctrine or scheme:

a)   which aims at the establishment of a despotic system of government based on the dictatorship of the proletariat under which one political organization only is recognized and all other political organizations are suppressed or eliminated; or

b)   which aims at bringing about any political, industrial, social or economic change within the Republic by the promotion of disturbance or disorder, by unlawful acts or omissions or by the threat of such acts or omissions; or

c)   which aims at bringing about any political, industrial, social or economic change within the Republic in accordance with the directions or under the guidance of or in cooperation with any foreign government or foreign or international institution whose purpose or one of whose purposes is to promote the establishment within the Republic of any system similar to that operating in any country which has adopted a system of government such as that described in paragraph (a); or

d)   which aims at the encouragement of feelings of hostility between the white and black races of the Republic the consequences of which are calculated to further the achievement of any object referred to in paragraph (a) or (b).

In terms of Section 2 of the Act, the Communist Party of S.A. was declared to be an unlawful organization. It was provided that the State President may, without notice to the organization concerned, by proclamation in the Gazette declare it to be an unlawful organization if he is satisfied that its purpose or one of its purposes is to promote the spread of communism or to further the achievements of any of the objects of communism, or is satisfied that it engages in activities which are calculated to further the achievement of any of the objects of communism, or that it carries on directly or indirectly any of the activities of an unlawful organization (Quoted from Horrell, SCA; SAIRR, May 1974)

BANNING ORDERS USUALLY MEAN:

a) For a period of five years (but sometimes two years), which may be repeated, the banned person is restricted to a particular magisterial district, or other specified area.

b) A prohibition on attendance at political gatherings, and frequently even social or family gatherings. (Two or more people appear to constitute a gathering.)

c) 'Listed' and 'banned' persons under the Act may not be office-bearers or members of political organizations, or of any of thirty-five organizations specifically listed in Government Notice No. 2130 of December 18, 1962; or of an unregistered trade union; or of any organization which defends, or attacks, or even discusses any form of State principle or policy; or of any organization which prepares, publishes or distributes any publication; or even an 'active supporter' of such an organization.

d) A banned person may be denied the right to be concerned in any way with the preparation of anything for printing or publication. He may be prevented from entering premises where a publication is produced.

e) He may not enter factory, trade union or mine premises, or railways, harbors or courts of law.

f) He may not enter African, Colored or Indian areas (unless as a Black person he is entering his 'own' area).

g) He may not communicate in anyway with another 'listed' or 'banned' person. Long friendships have been terminated by this provision, the penalty for non-observance being up to three years' imprisonment.

h) He may not give lectures or enter educational institutions; sometimes even a library is out of bounds.

i) Publication or reproduction of the speeches or writings (even after death) of a banned person is forbidden unless by way of evidence given in court, and then providing this does not afford 'a platform' for his views. This has meant that a banned person is unable to defend himself when attacked or smeared in public. It also means that a person's right to participate in the public life of the country is abolished.

j) A banned person must report weekly to a specified police station (sometimes daily).

k) If attempts to serve a banning order on an individual have proved unsuccessful, a copy affixed to the main entrance of the person's last known residence, and a notice in the

<u>Government Gazette</u> are deemed sufficient evidence that the notice has been served.

1) People listed, or convicted, under the Suppression of Communism Act are disqualified from practising as advocates, attorneys, notaries or conveyancers, unless the Minister agrees.

House Arrest

Occasionally a banning order includes house arrest, which imposes severe additional restrictions and which may be for twenty-four hours of the day, or for the overnight hours between 6 p.m. and 7 a.m., over weekends and public holidays. Under house arrest a person may receive no visitors other than a doctor or attorney (with the consent of the Minister). [(Quoted from "Sounds of Silence," Civil Rights League, May 1975).]

APPENDIX B.   THE NATIVE LAWS AMENDMENT ACT, 1952

Under the 1952 Native Laws Amendment Act the conditions under which an African can remain in an urban or proclaimed area are:

a)   He was born and permanently resides in such area; or

b)   He has worked continuously in such area for one employer for a period of not less than ten years or has lawfully remained continuously in such area for a period of not less than fifteen years and has not during either period been convicted of any offense in respect of which he has been sentenced to imprisonment without the option of a fine or a period of more than seven days or with the option of a fine for a period of more than one month; or

c)   Such Native is the wife, unmarried daughter or son under the age at which he would become liable for payment of general tax under the Natives Taxation and Development Act, 1925 (Act No. 41 of 1925) of any Native mentioned in paragraph (a) or (b) of this subsection, and ordinarily resides with that Native; or

d)   Permission so to remain has been granted to him by a person designated for the purpose by that local urban authority.

It is further provided in this Act that any authorized officer who 'has reason to believe' that any African (male or female) within an urban area is "idle, dissolute or disorderly" may "without warrant" arrest that African to be brought before a Native Commissioner or Magistrate. If the Native Commissioner or Magistrate declares the African "to be an idle or undesirable person" he may order that the African be removed from the urban area or be sent to a work colony or farm for employment...the Governor-General is empowered whenever he deems expedient and in the general public interest to order an African or a tribe to move from any part of the Union without the right to return unless given the written permission of the Secretary for Native Affairs. (Rule of Law, p. 30).

APPENDIX C. THE FREEDOM CHARTER, 1955

We the people of South Africa, declare for all our country and the world to know -

That South Africa belongs to all who live in it, black and white, and that no government can justly claim authority unless it is based on the will of all the people;

That our people have been robbed of their birthright to land, liberty and peace by a form of government founded on injustice and inequality;

That our country will never be prosperous or free until all our people live in brotherhood, enjoying equal rights and opportunities;

That only a democratic state, based on the will of all the people, can secure to all their birthright without distinction of color, race, sex or belief;

And therefore, we, the people of South Africa, black and white together - equals, countrymen and brothers - adopt this Freedom Charter. And we pledge ourselves to strive together, sparing nothing of our strength and courage, until the democratic changes here set out have been won.

THE PEOPLE SHALL GOVERN

Every man and woman shall have the right to vote for and to stand as a candidate for all bodies which make laws;

All people shall be entitled to take part in the administration of the country;

The rights of the people shall be the same, regardless of race, color or sex;

All bodies of minority rule, advisory boards, councils and authorities shall be replaced by democratic organs of self-government.

ALL NATIONAL GROUPS SHALL HAVE EQUAL RIGHTS

There shall be equal status in the bodies of state, in the courts and in the schools for all national groups and races;

All people shall have equal right to use their own languages and to develop their own folk culture and customs;

All national groups shall be protected by law against insults to their race and national pride;

The preaching and practice of national, race or color discrimination and contempt shall be a punishable crime;

All apartheid laws and practices shall be set aside.

THE PEOPLE SHALL SHARE IN THE COUNTRY'S WEALTH

The national wealth of our country, the heritage of all South Africans, shall be restored to the people;
The mineral wealth beneath the soil, the Banks and monopoly industry shall be transferred to the ownership of the people as a whole;
All other industry and trade shall be controlled to assist the well-being of the people;
All people shall have equal rights to trade where they choose, to manufacture and to enter all trades, crafts and professions.

THE LAND SHALL BE SHARED AMONG THOSE WHO WORK IT

Restriction of land ownership on a racial basis shall be ended, and all the land redivided amongst those who work it, to banish famine and land hunger;
The State shall help the peasant with implements, seed, tractors and dams to save the soil and assist the tillers;
Freedom of movement shall be guaranteed to all who work on the land;
All shall have the right to occupy land wherever they choose;
People shall not be robbed of their cattle, and forced labor and farm prisons shall be abolished.

ALL SHALL BE EQUAL BEFORE THE LAW

No-one shall be imprisoned, deported or restricted without a fair trial;
No-one shall be condemned by the order of any Government official;
The courts shall be representative of all the people;
Imprisonment shall be only for serious crimes against the people, and shall aim at re-education, not vengeance;
The police force and army shall be open to all on an equal basis and shall be the helpers and protectors of the people;
All laws which discriminate on grounds of race, color or belief shall be repealed.

ALL SHALL ENJOY EQUAL HUMAN RIGHTS

The law shall guarantee to all their right to speak, to organize, to meet together, to publish, to preach, to worship and to educate their children;
The privacy of the house from police raids shall be protected by law;
All shall be free to travel without restriction from

countryside to town, from province to province, and from South Africa abroad;

Pass Laws, permits and all other laws restricting these freedoms shall be abolished.

THERE SHALL BE WORK AND SECURITY

All who work shall be free to form trade unions, to elect their officers and to make wage agreements with their employers;

The State shall recognize the right and duty of all to work, and to draw full unemployment benefits;

Men and women of all races shall receive equal pay for equal work;

There shall be a forty-hour working week, a national minimum wage, paid annual leave, and sick leave for all workers, and maternity leave on full pay for all working mothers;

Miners, domestic workers, farm workers and civil servants shall have the same rights as all others who work;

Child labor, compound labor, the tot system and contract labor shall be abolished.

THE DOORS OF LEARNING AND OF CULTURE SHALL BE OPENED

The Government shall discover, develop and encourage national talent for the enhancement of our cultural life;

All the cultural treasures of mankind shall be open to all, by free exchange of books, ideas and contact with other lands;

The aim of education shall be to teach the youth to love their people and their culture, to honor human brotherhood, liberty and peace;

Education shall be free, compulsory, universal and equal for all children;

Higher education and technical training shall be opened to all by means of State allowances and scholarships awarded on the basis of merit;

Adult illiteracy shall be ended by a mass State education plan;

Teachers shall have all the rights of other citizens;

The color bar in cultural life, in sport and in education shall be abolished.

THERE SHALL BE HOUSES, SECURITY AND COMFORT

All people shall have the right to live where they choose, to be decently housed, and to bring up their families in comfort and security;

Unused housing space shall be made available to the people;

Rent and prices shall be lowered, food plentiful and no-one shall go hungry;

A preventive health scheme shall be run by the State;

Free medical care and hospitalization shall be provided for all, with special care for mothers and young children;

Slums shall be demolished, and new suburbs built where all have transport, roads, lighting, playing fields, creches and social centres;

The aged, the orphans, the disabled and the sick shall be cared for by the State;

Rest, leisure and recreation shall be the right of all;

Fenced locations and ghettoes shall be abolished, and laws which break up families shall be repealed.

THERE SHALL BE PEACE AND FRIENDSHIP

South Africa shall be a fully independent State, which respects the rights and sovereignity of all nations;

South Africa shall strive to maintain world peace and the settlement of all international disputes by negotiation - not war;

Peace and friendship amongst all our people shall be secured by upholding the equal rights, opportunities and status of all;

The people of the protectorates - Basutoland, Bechuanaland and Swaziland - shall be free to decide for themselves their own future;

The right of all the peoples of Africa to independence and self-government shall be recognized, and shall be the basis of close cooperation.

Let all who love their people and their country now say, as we say here: 'These freedoms we will fight for, side by side, throughout our lives, until we have won our liberty.'

CHAPTER 11

XI. STATISTICS

A. ELECTION RESULTS, 1920-1975

	Party	Number Seats	Number Votes	Prime Minister
1920	National Party	43	101,227	J.C. Smuts
	South African			
	National Party	41	90,512	(The South African
	Unionist	25	38,946	National and the
	Labor	21	40,639	Unionist Parites
	Independent	3	5,986	fused in November
				1920 to form the
				South African
				Party.)
1921	South African	77	137,389	J.C. Smuts
	National	44	105,039	
	Labor	10	29,406	
	Independent	1	3,385	
1924	National	63	111,483	J.B.M. Hertzog (The
	South African	54	148,769	National and Labor
	Labor	17	45,380	Parties formed the
	Independent	1	10,610	coalition "Pact"
				government.)
1929	National	77	141,579	J.B.M. Hertzog
	South African	61	159,896	
	Labor	8	33,919	
	Independent	1	8,503	
1933	National	75	101,159	J.B.M. Hertzog (In
	South African	61	71,486	1932 Hertzog and
	Labor	4	20,276	Smuts joined forces
	Home Rule	2	12,328	during the gold
	Independent	6	87,321	standard crisis.
	Roos	2	27,441	Only 34 percent of
				the registered
				voters voted in
				this election.
				White women were
				given the vote in
				1930.)

	Party	Number Seats	Number Votes	Prime Minister
1938	United Nat'l & S.Af.	111	446,032	J.B.M. Hertzog,
	National (Malan)	27	259,543	resigned after the
	Labor	3	48,641	War vote in 1939.
	Dominion	8	52,356	Died in 1942. J.C.
	Socialist	1	4,963	Smuts, 1939-1948.
	Native Reps. (1st)	3		
1943	United	85	435,297	J.C. Smuts
	National	43	321,601	
	Labor	9	38,206	
	Independent	2	30,185	
	Dominion	7	29,023	
	Native Reps.	3		
1948	National	70	401,834	Dr. Daniel F. Malan
	United	65	524,230	(The National and
	Afrikaner	9	41,885	Afrikaner Parties
	Labor	6	27,360	formed a coalition
	Native Reps.	3		in October 1951.)
	"Others"		70,662	
1953	National	94	598,718	Dr. Daniel F. Malan.
	United	57	576,474	Retired in November
	Labor	5	34,730	1954 at the age of 84.
	Native Reps (last)	3		J.G. Strijdom, 1954-
				1958.
1958	National	103	642,069	J.G. Strijdom. Died 1958.
	United	53	503,639	Dr. H.F. Verwoerd,
	Coloreds' Reps (1st)	4		1958-1966.
1961	National	105	370,431	Dr. H.F. Verwoerd
	United	49	302,875	
	National Union	1	35,903	
	Progressive	1	69,042	
	Coloreds' Reps.	4		
1966	National	126	58.6 percent of total vote	Dr. H.F. Verwoerd. Assassinated September 1966.
	United	39	37.1 percent	
	Progressive	1	3.1	B.J. Vorster (Prime Minister and Minister of Police) 1966 to the present.

October 5, 1960 Republican Referendum Vote

	FOR	AGAINST
Cape	271,418	269,784
Transvaal	406,632	325,041
Natal	42,299	135,598
Orange Free State	110,171	33,438
South West Africa	19,938	12,017
Total	850,458	775,878

B. GROSS DOMESTIC PRODUCT (R million) 1912-1966

	Agriculture Forestry and Fishing	Mining/ Quarrying	Manuftg.	Wholesale/ Retail	Other	Total
1912	66.3	80.9	13.1	40.3	106.6	307.2
1920	122.1	94.8	40.6	86.2	201.4	545.1
1930	77.9	81.7	50.9	82.3	248.7	541.5
1940	119.9	185.0	121.9	136.5	413.0	976.3
1950	432.3	326.3	417.5	350.6	965.4	2492.1
1960	587.7	656.0	915.5	632.1	2021.3	4812.6
1966	820.0	968.0	1721.0	1081.0	3332.0	7922.0

(1969 Yearbook, page 250)

C. PERCENT CONTRIBUTION TO THE GROSS DOMESTIC PRODUCT 1912-1966

	Agriculture	Mining	Manufacturing	Commerce
1912	21.6	26.3	4.3	13.1
1920	22.4	17.4	7.4	15.8
1930	14.4	15.1	9.4	15.2
1940	12.3	18.9	12.5	14.0
1950	17.3	13.1	16.8	14.1
1960	12.2	13.6	19.0	13.1
1966	10.3	12.2	21.7	13.6

(1969 Yearbook, page 250)

D. OCCUPATIONS: BY MAIN SECTORS, RACE AND SEX 1960 AND 1951

1960
MALES (THOUSANDS)

	Whites	Africans	Colored people	Asians	All races	Per-centage
Agriculture, forestry and fishing	114	1302[+]	114	9	1539	35
Mining	59	538	4	--	601	14
Manufacturing	183	304	62	30	579	13
Construction	70	164	40	2	276	6
Electricity, gas and water	10	25	3	--	38	1
Commerce and finance	131	149	33	26	339	8
Transport and communications	106	71	17	4	198	5
Services	147	304	41	19	511	11
Unemployed	28	202	56	23	309	7
Total economically active (a)	849	3059	369	113	4390	100
Total population (b)	1539	5503	751	241	8034	
(a) as percentage of (b)	(55)	(55)	(49)	(47)	(53)	

115

1951
MALES (THOUSANDS)

	Whites	Africans	Colored people	Asians	All races	Per- centage
Agriculture, forestry and fishing	141	1158[+]	94	12	1406	38
Mining	55	448	4	1	507	14
Manufacturing	143	221	45	20	429	12
Construction	66	132	39	2	238	6
Electricity, gas and water	7	17	2	--	25	1
Commerce and finance	109	99	23	22	253	7
Transport and communications	103	73	14	2	192	5
Services	124	285	33	15	456	12
Unemployed	21[‡]	112[‡]	33	13	179	5
Total economically active (a)	769[§]	2542[§]	286[§]	88[§]	3685[§]	100
Total population (b)	1323	4369	551	190	6432	
(a) as percentage of (b)	(58)	(53)	(52)	(47)	(57)	

116

FEMALES (THOUSANDS)

	Whites	Africans	Colored people	Asians	All races	Per- centage
Agriculture, forestry and fishing	4	149	5	1	160	12
Mining	3	1	--	--	4	--
Manufacturing	46	16	35	3	100	8
Construction	2	--	--	--	2	--
Electricity, gas and water	1	--	--	--	1	--
Commerce and finance	102	8	6	2	118	9
Transport and communications	16	--	--	--	16	1
Services	105	509	100	4	719	55
Unemployed	14	133	33	4	184	14
Total economically active (a)	292	818	179	13	1302	100
Total population (b)	1549	5404	758	235	7946	
(a) as percentage of (b)	(19)	(15)	(23)	(5)	(16)	

FEMALES (THOUSANDS)

	Whites	Africans	Colored people	Asians	All races	Per- centage
Agriculture, forestry and fishing	4	94	4	1	103	11
Mining	2	1	--	--	3	--
Manufacturing	40	7	26	2	73	8
Construction	1	--	--	--	2	--
Electricity, gas and water	--	--	--	--	--	--
Commerce and finance	70	2	2	1	75	9
Transport and communications	11	--	--	--	11	1
Services	80	456	79	2	617	68
Unemployed	7‡	6‡	9‡	1‡	23	3
Total economically active (a)	215§	567§	119§	7§	907	100
Total population (b)	1318	4191	552	177	6239	
(a) as percentage of (b)	(16)	(14)	(22)	(4)	(15)	

(D. Hobart Houghton, The South African Economy, p. 256-257.)

E. EMPLOYMENT AND EARNINGS 1950, 1960, 1970

		Mining	Manufacturing	Construction	Transport	Public authorities
Number of workers (all races)(thousands)	1950	503,3	486,3	77,8	187,9	--
"	1960	620,1	615,7	114,5	218,0	510,3
"	1970	675,8	1171,3	367,8	232,3	645,1
Earnings (all races)(R millions)	1950	125,4	240,8	34,2	129,0	--
"	1960	249,0	496,1	77,6	217,2	445,7
"	1970	410,9	1636,6	450,8	474,7	1028,0
Average earnings per worker (R p.a.)	1950	249,2	514,2	439,6	686,5	--
"	1960	401,5	805,7	677,7	996,3	873,4
"	1970	608,0	1397,3	1225,7	2043,5	1593,6
Number of white workers (thousands)	1950	55,9	155,1	19,1	103,3	--
"	1960	67,7	162,8	22,9	110,0	205,7
"	1970	62,5	275,4	60,5	110,7	238,0
Earnings of white workers (R millions)	1950	79,8	151,1	20,2	105,9	--
"	1960	156,5	313,7	42,8	185,3	334,0
"	1970	273,1	1003,4	231,9	402,4	769,6
Average earnings of white workers (R p.a.)	1950	1427,5	974,2	1057,6	1025,2	--
"	1960	2311,7	1926,9	1870,0	1684,5	1623,7
"	1970	4369,6	3643,4	3833,1	3635,1	3233,6
Number of colored workers (thousands)	1950	2,5	69,7	7,9	9,7	--
"	1960	3,9	87,3	15,8	9,7	38,7
"	1970	6,5	196,1	45,5	14,3	60,8
Earnings of colored workers (R millions)	1950	--	26,1	3,7	--	--
"	1960	--	49,2	10,5	--	28,6
"	1970	5,6	172,2	59,2	--	69,6
Average earnings of colored workers (Rp.a.)	1950	--	374,4	468,4	--	--
"	1960	--	563,6	664,6	--	739,0
"	1970	875,0	878,1	1301,1	--	1144,7

		Mining	Manu-facturing	Con-struction	Trans-port	Public author-ities
Number of Asian workers (thousands)	1950	0,6	19,6	0,2	0,6	--
"	1960	0,5	29,2	0,6	0,6	7,5
"	1970	0,6	75,1	4,4	1,2	13,7
Earnings of Asian workers (R millions)	1950	--	7,5	0,1	--	--
"	1960	--	17,3	0,6	--	6,0
"	1970	0,7	70,3	8,1	--	18,0
Average earnings of Asians workers (R p.a.)	1950	--	382,7	500,0	--	--
"	1960	--	592,5	1000,0	--	800,0
"	1970	1166,7	936,1	1840,9	--	1313,8
Number of African workers (thousands)	1950	444,2	241,8	50,5	74,2	--
"	1960	547,9	336,3	75,0	96,6	258,1
"	1970	606,2	624,6	257,4	97,1	332,5
Earnings of African workers (R millions)	1950	--	56,1	10,3	--	--
"	1960	--	115,9	23,6	--	77,1
"	1970	131,5	391,2	151,6	--	170,8
Average earnings of African workers (Rp.a.)	1950	--	232,0	204,0	--	--
"	1960	--	344,6	314,7	--	298,7
"	1970	216,9	626,3	589,0	--	513,7
Number of non-white workers (thousands)	1950	447,4	--	--	84,6	--
"	1960	552,4	--	--	108,0	--
"	1970	613,3	--	--	121,6	--
Earnings of non-white workers (R millions)	1950	45,6	--	--	23,1	--
"	1960	92,5	--	--	31,9	--
"	1970	137,8	--	--	72,3	--
Average earnings of non-white workers (Rpa)	1950	98,1	--	--	273,0	--
"	1960	167,5	--	--	295,4	--
"	1970	224,7	--	--	594,6	--

(D. Hobart Houghton, The South African Economy, p. 274)

120

F.   GROWTH OF PRIVATE MANUFACTURING INDUSTRY 1925-70

Year ending June	Number of establishments	Total employment (thousands)	Value of gross output (R millions)	Value of net output (R millions)
1925	6009	115	115	49
1939	8614	236	281	128
1945	9316	361	608	276
1946	9642	379	669	305
1947	9999	397	780	347
1948	11376	434	922	401
1949	12060	473	1062	457
1950	12517	498	1217	512
1951	12983	543	1583	622
1952	12887	576	1809	700
1953	13260	596	1908	775
1954	13881	622	2013	860
1955[+]	13725	652	2221	964
1955[+]	10128	616	2154	852
1956	10378	640	2334	907
1957	10291	661	2465	980
1958	10640	676	2603	1033
1959	10967	677	2650	1058
1960	11411	668	2792	1129
1961	11885	689	3024	1228
1962	12514	709	3220	1329
1963	11985	767	3518	1442
1964	11944	826	4045	1641
1966	12727	937	5104	2038
1968	13142	989	5983	2393
1970	---	1164	7370	2908

[+]Figures are comparable to 1955 when some repair units and workshops were removed. The second set of figures for 1955 is comparable with latter years.

(D. Hobart Houghton, The South African Economy, p. 271.)

G. POPULATION BY RACE, 1921–1960

	Total	White	African	Asian	Colored
1904	5,174,827	1,117,234	3,490,291	122,311	444,991
1921	6,927,403	1,521,343	4,697,285	163,594	545,181
1936	9,587,863	2,003,334	6,595,597	219,691	769,241
1946	11,415,925	2,372,044	7,830,559	285,260	928,062
1951	12,671,452	2,641,689	8,560,083	366,664	1,103,016
1960	15,982,664	3,088,492	10,907,789	477,125	1,509,258

(1969 Yearbook, p. 61)

H. PERCENT POPULATION BY RACE IN URBAN AND RURAL AREAS, 1911–1960

	URBAN				RURAL			
	White	African	Colored	Asian	White	African	Colored	Asian
1911	51.6	12.6		45.9	48.4	87.4		54.1
1921	55.8	12.5	45.8	20.9	44.2	87.5	54.2	69.1
1936	65.2	17.3	53.9	66.3	34.8	82.7	46.1	33.7
1946	73.4	23.1	58.9	70.7	26.6	76.9	41.1	29.3
1951	79.1	27.9	66.2	77.6	20.9	72.1	33.8	22.4
1960	83.6	31.8	68.3	83.2	16.4	28.2	31.7	16.8

I. MISCELLANEOUS

1. Defense Expenditures

1960 - 61	R 45.8 million
1966 - 67	R 256 million
1975	R 900 million

2. Telephone Exchange Connections

	1938-39	1945-46	1965-66
Business	59,693	78,836	207,808
Residence	63,748	91,221	417,688

(1969 Yearbook)

3. Radio Listeners' Licenses Issued

1930	25,121	1960	999,358
1940	283,119	1967	1,588,739
1950	554,863		

(1969 Yearbook)

4. Number of Posts in the Civil Service

1939	1950	1960	1967
57,025	106,956	148,592	212,788

(1969 Yearbook)

5. Expenditures for Education (Government)

a. Per Pupil

	White	Asian (and) Colored		African
1940	R 52.8	R 11.4		R 4.4
1950	100.2	34.8		15.2
1968	228	R 70	R 73	14.5

b. Total (R millions)

	White	Asian (and) Colored	African
1910	R 3.2	---	R 0.2
1920	12.6	---	0.6
1930	16.8	R 1.0	1.2
1940	21.4	2.0	2.0
1950	50.8	9.4	11.6

(van den Berghe, p. 298)

CHAPTER 12

BIBLIOGRAPHY

1. MAIN SOURCES

Periodicals, Yearbooks, Reports and Newspapers

The African Communist, 1959-1967.

Cape Times, 1930-1970.

Church of the Province of South Africa. Seek, 1960-1975.
    Proceedings, 1930-1968.

The Garment Worker, 1950s.

Government Publications, South African Digest, 1964-1975.

The Guardian, 1937-1952. Banned.
    Clarion, 1952. Banned.
    Advance, 1952-1954. Banned.
    New Age, 1954-1960. Banned.
    Spark, 1961-1963. Staff banned.

Inkululeko, 1940-1950.

International Commission of Jurists. Bulletin. (Published
    periodically with sections on South Africa.)

Rand Daily Mail, 1920-1970.

Sechaba, 1968-1974 (ANC)

South African Institute of Race Relations.
    Annual Report, 1930-1975.
    Race Relations News, 1960-1975.

The South African Worker, 1921-1930.

SPRO-CAS Publications.
    Some Implications of Inequality (1971).
    South Africa's Minorities (1971).
    Anatomy of Apartheid (1970).
    Directions of Change in South African Politics (1971).
    Education beyond Apartheid, Report of the Education Commission
        (1971).
    South Africa's Political Alternatives, Report of the Political
        Commission (1973).

Towards Social Change, Report of the Social Commission (1971).
Apartheid and the Church, Report of the Church Commission
    (1972).
Power, Privilege, and Poverty, Report of the Economics
    Commission (1972).

State of South Africa,
    Economic, Financial and Statistical Year-Book for the Republic
    of South Africa. Johannesburg: Da Gama, 1969.

Umsebenzi, 1930-1938.

Yearbook of the Union and of the Republic of South Africa, 1925-1969.

Personal Interviews with
    Mary Benson
    Hilda Watts Bernstein
    Arthur Blaxall
    Brian Bunting
    Bettie du Toit
    Trevor Huddleston
    Ambrose Reeves
    E.S. Sachs
    Michael Scott

                    Books, Brochures, and Articles

African Taxation. Its Relation to African Social Services.
    Johannesburg: SAIRR, 1960.

Alexander, Ray and Simons, H.J. "Job Reservation and the Trade
    Unions." Cape Town: Enterprise, 1959.

Altman, Phyllis. The Law of the Vultures. London: Jonathan
    Cape, 1952.

Benson, Mary. The African Patriots. The Story of the African
    National Congress of South Africa. N.Y.: Encyclopedia
    Britannica, 1964. (First American Edition).

Bernstein, Hilda. The World That Was Ours. London: Heineman,
    1967.

Blumberg, Myrna. White Madam. London: Gollancz, 1962.

Bunting, Brian. The Rise of the South African Reich.
    Baltimore, Md.: Penguin, 1964.

Civil Rights League. "Sounds of Silence. The Rule of Law in
    Relation to the Banning System under SCA." Cape Town:
    League, 1975.

Cope, John. South Africa. N.Y.: Praeger, 1965.

de Gruchy, Joy. The Cost of Living for Urban Africans.
Johannesburg: SAIRR, 1960.

Feit, Edward. South Africa, The Dynamics of the African
National Congress. London: Oxford, 1962.

(Feit, Edward.) Workers without Weapons: the South African
Congress of Trade Unions and the organization of the African
workers. Hamden, Conn.: Archon Books, 1975.

Gardiner, Gerald. The South African Treason Trial. London:
Christian Action, 1957.

Garment Workers in Action, 1928-1952. Johannesburg: Eagle, 1957.
198 pp.

Hellmann, Ellen & Abrahams, Leah. Handbook on Race Relations in
South Africa. Cape Town: Oxford, 1949.

Hellmann, Ellen. Sellgoods. A Sociological Survey of an African
Commercial Labor Force. Johannesburg: SAIRR, 1953.

(Hellmann, Ellen.) Soweto, Johannesburg's African City.
Johannesburg: SAIRR, 1971.

Hepple, Alex. South Africa, A Political and Economic History.
N.Y.: Praeger, 1966.

(Hepple, Alex.) Trade Union in Travail. Johannesburg: Unity,
1954.

Herd, Norman. 1922. The Revolt on the Rand. Johannesburg:
Blue Cnane, 1966.

Hooper, Charles. Brief Authority. London: Collins, 1960.

Horrell, Muriel. Action, Reaction, and Counteraction. Johannesburg: Institute of Race Relations, 1963.

(Horrell, Muriel.) "Facts and Figures - Non-White Labor."
Johannesburg: Institute of Race Relations, 1964.

(Horrell, Muriel.) Group Areas, The Emerging Pattern. Johannesburg: Institute of Race Relations, 1966.

(Horrell, Muriel.) Legislation and Race Relations. Johannesburg:
Institute of Race Relations, 1966. (Revised Edition).

(Horrell, Muriel.) Racialism and the Trade Unions. Johannesburg:
Institute of Race Relations, 1959.

(Horrell, Muriel.) The Rights of African Women: Some suggested
    Reforms. Johannesburg: Institute of Race Relations, 1971.

(Horrell, Muriel.) South African Trade Unionism, a Study of a
    Divided Working Class. Johannesburg: Institute of Race
    Relations, 1961.

(Horrell, Muriel.) South Africa's Non-White Workers. Johannesburg:
    Institute of Race Relations, 1956.

(Horrell, Muriel.) "Suppression of Communism Act: Notes on action
    taken against persons." Johannesburg: Institute of Race
    Relations, 1974.

(Horrell, Muriel.) A Survey of Race Relations in South Africa.
    Annually from 1949 to the present. Johannesburg: Institute
    of Race Relations, 1949-1975.

Horwitz, Ralph. The Political Economy of South Africa. New York:
    Praeger, 1967.

Houghton, D. Hobart. Economic Development in a Plural Society.
    Studies in the Border Region of the Cape Province. Cape
    Town: Oxford, 1960.

(Houghton, D. Hobart.) The South African Economy. Cape Town:
    Oxford, 1973. (Third Edition).

Johns, Sheridan Waite. Marxism – Leninism in a Multi-Racial Society:
    the origin and early history of the Communist Party of South
    Africa, 1914-1933. Cambridge: Harvard, 1965. (ph.D.
    Dissertation)

Joseph, Helen. If This Be Treason. London: Deutsch, 1963.

Joseph, Helen. Tomorrow's Sun, A smuggled journal from South
    Africa. New York: John Day, 1967.

Joshi, P.S. Unrest in South Africa. Bombay: Hind Kitabs Ltd.,
    1953.

Kadalie, Clements (edited by S. Trapido). My Life and the ICU,
    The Autobiography of a Black Trade Unionist in South Africa.
    New York: Humanities, 1970. 239 pp.

Kruger, D.W., editor. South African Parties and Policies, 1910-1960.
    New York: International Publications, 1960.

Kuper, Leo. An African Bourgeousie. New Haven: Yale, 1965.

(Kuper, Leo.) Passive Resistance in South Africa. New Haven:
    Yale, 1960.

Legum, Colin and Margaret. South Africa: Crisis for the West. New York: Praeger, 1964.

Lerumo, A. Fifty Fighting Years, The Communist Party of South Africa, 1921-1971. London: Inkululeko, 1971.

Lever, Henry. The South African Voter. Cape Town: Juta, 1972.

Longmore, Laura. The Dispossessed: A study of the sex-life of Bantu women in urban areas in and around Johannesburg. London: Jonathan Cape, 1959.

Marquard, Leo. The Peoples and Policies of South Africa. Cape Town: Oxford, 1960. (Second Edition).

Mayer, Philip. Townsmen or Tribesmen. Conservatism and the Process of Urbanization in a South African City. Cape Town: Oxford, 1971. (Second Edition).

Mbeki, Govan. South Africa: The Peasants' Revolt. Baltimore, Md.: Penguin, 1964.

Pauw, B.A. Religion in a Tswana Chiefdom. London: Oxford, 1960.

(Pauw, B.A.) Xhosa in Town: The Second Generation. Cape Town: Oxford, 1963.

Roux, Edward. S.P. Bunting. A Political Biography. Cape Town: African Bookman, 1943.

(Roux, Edward.) Time Longer than Rope. A History of the Black Man's Struggle for Freedom in South Africa. London: Victor Gollancz, Ltd., 1949.

Sachs, Albie. Justice in South Africa. Los Angeles: University of California, 1973.

Sachs, E.S. The Choice before South Africa. London: the author, 1953.

(Sachs, E.S.) Rebel Daughters. London: Macgibbon and Kee, 1957.

Sachs, E.S. and Forman, Lionel. The South African Treason Trial. New York: Monthly Review Press, 1958.

Simons, Jack and Ray. Class and Color in South Africa, 1850-1950. Harmondsworth: Penguin, 1969.

Sampson, Anthony. The Treason Cage. London: Heinemann, 1958.

Stultz, Newell M. Afrikaner Politics in South Africa, 1934-1948. Los Angeles: University of California, 1974.

van den Berghe, Pierre L. South Africa, A Study in Conflict.
    Middletown, Connecticut: Wesleyan, 1965.

Vermaak, Christopher Johann. The Red Trap: Communism and Violence
    in South Africa. Johannesburg: A.P.B., 1966.

(Various Authors) "The Western Areas Removal Scheme." Johannesburg:
    Institute of Race Relations, 1953.

Weyl, Nathaniel. Traitors' End. The Rise and Fall of the Communist
    Movement in Southern Africa. Cape Town: Tafelberg-Uitgewers,
    1970.

Walker, Ivan L. and Weinbren, B. 2000 Casualties: A History of the
    Trade Unions and the Labor Movement in the Union of South
    Africa. Johannesburg: South African Trade Union Council, 1961.

Walshe, Peter. The Rise of African Nationalism in South Africa.
    The African National Congress, 1912-1952. Los Angeles:
    University of California, 1971.

Whitfield, George M. South African Native Law. Cape Town: Juta,
    1948. (Second Edition).

Wilson, Francis and Perrot, Dominique. Outlook on a Century:
    South Africa 1870-1970. Lovedale and Christian Institute/
    SPRO-CAS, 1975.

Wix, Ethel. The Cost of Living. Johannesburg: Institute of Race
    Relations, 1951.

2. SUPPLEMENTAL SOURCES

Books, Articles, and Brochures

Amnesty International. Prison Conditions in South Africa. London:
    AI, 1965.

Andrews, H.T. et alia, editors. South Africa in the Sixties, a
    Socio-Economic Survey. Cape Town: South Africa Foundation,
    1965. (Second Revised Edition).

Arkin, Marcus. "Strikes, Boycotts - and the History of their
    Impact on South Africa." South African Journal of Economics
    (December 1960) vol. 28, no. 4, pp. 303-318.

Carter, Gwendolen M. The Politics of Inequality: South Africa
    since 1948. London: Thames and Hudson, 1958.

Civil Rights League. "The Power to Arrest and the Rights of
    Arrested Persons in South Africa." Cape Town: Institute of
    Race Relations, 1966.

Davies, Joan. *African Trade Unions*. Baltimore, Md.: Penguin, 1966.

de Kiewiet, C.W. *A History of South Africa*, Social and Economic. Oxford: Clarendon, 1941.

de Villiers, C.F.; Metrowich, F.R.; du Plessis, J.A. *The Communist Strategy*. Pretoria: Department of Information, 1975.

Dison, L.R. and Mohamed, I. *Group Areas and Their Development*, including Land Tenure and Occupation. Durban: Butterworths, 1960.

Douwes Dekker, L.C.G. "Are Works Committees Trade Unions?" Johannesburg: Institute of Race Relations, 1973.

Encyclopedia of Southern Africa. Compiled and edited by Eric Rosenthal. New York: Frederick Warne, 1970. (Fifth Edition).

Friedland, William H. *Unions, Labor and Industrial Relations in Africa*, an Annotated Bibliography. Ithaca: Cornell, 1965.

Gordon, Mira. "Trade Unionism in South Africa, 1952-1966. A Select Bibliography." Johannesburg: University of the Witwatersrand, 1968.

Haldane, Richard M. "The Unique Basis of Trade Unions in South Africa." *Optima* (September 1961) pp. 152-157.

Hartmann, Heinz. *Enterprise and Politics in South Africa*. Princeton: Princeton, 1962.

Hepple, Alex. *The African Worker in South Africa*: A Study in Trade Unionism. London: Africa Bureau, 1956.

(Hepple, Alex.) *A Trade Union Guide for South African Workers*. Johannesburg: SACTU, 1957.

History Speaks for Freedom. From protest to challenge. 1882-1964. Documents of African Politics in South Africa. Stanford: Hoover Institute, 1973.

Hoagland, Jim. *South Africa*, Civilizations in Conflict. Boston: Houghton Mifflin, 1972.

Horrell, Muriel. *Introduction to South Africa*. Basic Facts and Figures. Johannesburg: Institute of Race Relations, 1968.

Hurwitz, Nathan. *The Economics of Bantu Education in South Africa*. Johannesburg: Institute of Race Relations, 1964.

Hutt, W.H. *The Economics of the Color Bar*. A study of the Economic Origins and Consequences of Racial Segregation in South Africa. London: Andre Deutsch, 1964.

130

Industrial and Commercial Workers' Union of Africa. Economic and
    Wages Commission: Evidence Submitted at Johannesburg on 19th
    September, 1925. Johannesburg: ICU, 1925.

International Commission of Jurists. The Rule of Law in South
    Africa. Geneva: International Commission of Jurists, 1960.

International Labor Office. Apartheid, Development of the Situa-
    tion in the Republic of South Africa. Geneva: ILD, 1965.

International Labor Organization. "Declaration concerning the
    Policy of Apartheid of the Republic of South Africa," and
    "I.L.O. Programme for the Elimination of Apartheid in Labor
    Matters in the Republic of South Africa." Geneva: ILO, 1964.

International Labor Organization. "Special Report of the Director-
    General on the Application of the Declaration concerning the
    Policy of Apartheid of the Republic of South Africa."
    International Labor Conference, 49th Session, Geneva, 1965.
    Geneva: ILO, 1965. Second Special Report...50th Session,
    Geneva, 1966.

Kahn, Ellison. "The Right to Strike in South Africa." South
    African Journal of Economics (March 1943) Vol. II, no. 1,
    pp. 24-27.

Letsoaba, J. "The Fight for Trade Union Rights in South Africa."
    London: Union of Democratic Control, n.d.

Little, Kenneth. African Women in Towns: An aspect of Africa's
    social revolution. London: Oxford, 1973.

Lynd, G.E. The Politics of African Trade Unionism. New York:
    Praeger, 1968.

Mandela, Nelson. No Easy Walk to Freedom. London: 1965.

Mathews, Anthony S. Law, Order and Liberty in South Africa.
    Los Angeles: University of California, 1972.

Meynaud, J. and Bey, A.S. Trade Unionism in Africa: A Study of
    its Growth and Orientation. New York: Barnes, 1967.

Molteno, Donald B. "The Assault on our Liberties, the State of
    Civil Rights in South Africa." Johannesburg: Institute of
    Race Relations, 1958.

Mtolo, Bruno. Umkhonto we Sizwe, The Road to the Left. Durban:
    Drakensburg, 1966.

Muller, Andre Loedolff. Minority Interests: the political economy
    of the Colored and Indian communities in South Africa.
    Johannesburg: Institute of Race Relations, 1968.

Orde Brown, G.S.   The African Laborer.   London: Cass, 1967.

Piercy, Mary V.   "Statutory Work Reservation."   South African
     Journal of Economics (June 1960) vol. 28, no. 2 pp. 119-140,
     and (September 1960) vol. 28, no. 3, p. 206-233.

Political Africa.   A Who's Who of Personalities and Parties.
     Ronald Segal.   New York: Praeger, 1961.

Report of the Group of Experts established in pursuance of the
     Security Council resolution of 4 December 1963.   "A New
     Course in South Africa."   New York: United Nations, n.d.

Robertson, H.M.   South Africa: Economic and Political Aspects.
     Durham, N.C.:   Duke, 1957.

Routh, Guy.   Industrial Relations and Race Relations.   Johannesburg:
     Institute of Race Relations, n.d.

Schaeffer, M.   The Industrial Conciliation Act, number 36 of 1937,
     together with the Regulations published under Government Notice
     number 1841, dated 2nd December, 1937.   Cape Town: Juta, 1938.

Scott, Michael.   A Time to Speak.   London: 1958.

South African Prospects and Progress.   New York: South African
     Information Service, 1969.

South African Trade Union Council.   "Memorandum Submitted to the
     Select Committee appointed to enquire into the Industrial
     Conciliation Bill (A.B. 1953-1954)."   Durban: SATUC, 1954.
     "Supplementary Memorandum."   Durban: SATUC, 1955.

South African Trades and Labor Council, "Minutes of the Special
     Conference on the Industrial Legislation Commission's Report."
     Johannesburg: South African Trades and Labor Council, 1952.

South African Trades and Labor Council.   "Strike of the 60,000
     African Mine-workers on the Witwatersrand Gold Mines."
     Johannesburg: South African Trades and Labor Council, 1947.

Spooner, F.P.   The South African Predicament, the Economics of
     Apartheid.   London: Jonathan Cape, 1960.

Suzman, Arthur.   "Race Classification and Definition in the
     Legislation of the Union of South Africa, 1910-1960."   A
     Survey and Analysis.   Johannesburg: Institute of Race Relations,
     1960.

Troup, Freda.   South Africa, an Historical Introduction.   London:
     Eyre Methuen, 1972.

Ushpol, Rowse. *A Select Bibliography of South African Autobiographies*. Cape Town: University, 1956.

van der Horst, Sheila. *Native Labor in South Africa*. London: Oxford, 1942.

Wilson, Francis. *Migrant Labor in South Africa*. Johannesburg: South African Council of Churches, 1972.